MW00629676

METAPHYSICS AS A PERSONAL ADVENTURE

Christos Yannaras in Conversation with Norman Russell

St Vladimir's Seminary Press

ORTHODOX CHRISTIAN PROFILES SERIES

Number 9

The Orthodox Christian Profiles Series acquaints the reader on an intimate level with Orthodox figures that have shaped the direction of the Orthodox Church in areas of mission, ascetical and liturgical theology, scholarly and pastoral endeavors, and various other professional disciplines. The people featured in the series are mostly our contemporaries and most remain active in shaping the life of the Church today. A few will have fallen asleep in the Lord, but their influence remains strong and worthy of historical record. The mission of this series is to introduce inspirational Orthodox Christian leaders in various ministries and callings that build up the Body of Christ.

Chad Hatfield
Series Editor

Metaphysics as a Personal Adventure

CHRISTOS YANNARAS
in Conversation with
NORMAN RUSSELL

ST VLADIMIR'S SEMINARY PRESS
YONKERS, NY 10707
2017

Library of Congress Cataloging-in-Publication Data

Names: Russell, Norman, 1945– author, interviewer. | Giannaras, Chrēstos,
  1935– interviewee.
Title: Metaphysics as a Personal Adventure : Christos Yannaras in
  conversation with Norman Russell / Norman Russell.
Description: Yonkers, NY : St Vladimir's Seminary Press, 2017. | Series:
  Orthodox Christian profiles series ; number 9 | Includes bibliographical
  references.
Identifiers: LCCN 2017008570 (print) | LCCN 2017012936 (ebook) | ISBN
  9780881415834 () | ISBN 9780881415827 (paper) | ISBN 9780881415834
  (electronic)
Subjects: LCSH: Metaphysics. | Ontology. | Giannaras, Chrēstos, 1935– |
  Orthodox Eastern Church—Doctrines.
Classification: LCC BD111 (ebook) | LCC BD111 .R877 2017 (print) | DDC
  230/.19092—dc23
LC record available at https://lccn.loc.gov/2017008570

COPYRIGHT © 2017
ST VLADIMIR'S SEMINARY PRESS
575 Scarsdale Rd, Yonkers, NY 10707
1–800–204–2665
www.svspress.com

ISBN 978–0-88141–582–7 (paper)
ISBN 978–0-88141–583–4 (electronic)

PRINTED IN THE UNITED STATES OF AMERICA

To Nikos Mouyiaris

Contents

Preface

I had been translating the work of Christos Yannaras for some years without actually having met him. We had spoken on the telephone and corresponded, but until 2010 we had not come together face-to-face. In November of that year, I was invited to attend a conference in Athens. I saw this as a wonderful opportunity to arrange a meeting, and was disappointed to find that he was away in Istanbul on a visit to the Ecumenical Patriarch. He was flying back, however, on the day I was due to leave, and his secretary told me he was determined not to miss the chance of seeing me. He came straight from the airport to the hotel where I was staying. We met in the foyer and for a brief moment gazed at each other, recollecting the years that had passed and the work we had done together. Then we fell into each other's arms and wept. We talked nonstop in the hotel, in the car back to the airport, and at the airport itself until I passed reluctantly through the gates to take my flight. I was already familiar with the clarity of Yannaras's thinking, but this was my first experience of the extraordinary warmth of the man himself.

The conversation we began on that day has continued in correspondence and in subsequent meetings. One of my early mentors was Fr Louis Bouyer, who had the same ability as Christos Yannaras to communicate complex thoughts in lively, intimate conversation. A book of Bouyer's that had particularly impressed me was his *Le métier de théologien: entretiens avec Georges Daix* (Paris, 1979), the record of an extended interview in which Bouyer talked about his work and the way he conceived of the theologian's task. It occurred to me that a similar format might enable Yannaras to respond to some of the questions asked about his work, and indeed to answer objections often raised against it, for like Bouyer, Yannaras sees theology—along with philosophy—not as an academic enterprise, but as an approach to reality in all the dimensions vital to our life today. We began a series of e-mails, with my posing questions and his replying and commenting. The result, translated into English and lightly edited, is the present volume.

I should like to thank Fr Chad Hatfield for accepting this book so readily in the Profiles series of St Vladimir's Seminary Press. It is a sign of the increasing recognition of Yannaras's work in the English-speaking world that it is no longer necessary to go cap-in-hand from one publisher to another in search of one that will undertake the financial risk of publication. There is no hiding the fact that, for many, Yannaras is a controversial figure. He castigates much of what passes for Christianity today, in the East as well as in the West. But his focus is not narrowly ecclesiastical. In his writings he confronts, directly or indirectly, many of the wider problems that afflict us today—"the threat to the environment, the assimilation of politics to business models, the yawning gulf between society and the state, the pursuit of ever-greater consumption, the loneliness and weakness of social relations, the prevailing loveless sexuality" (*Orthodoxy and the West*, ix)—all of which he shows to be grounded in theological issues. Even at the beginning of his ninth decade, he remains a prophetic voice for the twenty-first century.

Norman Russell
Ozenay, July 2016

Introduction

One evening in the fall of 1964, a long train drew out of Athens Larissa Station bound for Munich. In the train was a carriage fitted with couchettes that the West German government had supplied for a group of Greek students from various disciplines who had been awarded scholarships for postgraduate study in the Federal Republic of Germany. Among these students was Christos Yannaras. There was excitement in the air. Intense conversations went on late into the night. The students knew how important this venture was, not just for equipping them for their subsequent careers, but for the exposure it offered them to the academic culture of Western Europe.

Early Life and Studies Abroad

Yannaras had been awarded a scholarship by the Alexander von Humboldt Foundation, which supported him for two of the three years he was to spend at Bonn. Born in Athens in 1935, he spent his formative years in Greece. After graduating in theology from the University of Athens in 1964, he decided on an academic career, which in those days required a period of study abroad. With the opportunity offered by the Humboldt scholarship, he embarked on what was to be a very fruitful phase of postgraduate research.

In Germany, at the University of Bonn, Yannaras discovered Heidegger, whose critique of the Western metaphysical tradition was a revelation to him and was to color the whole of his life's work. Heidegger showed how a metaphysics that identified reality with its intellectual signification led inexorably to a Hegelian metaphysics of absolute subjectivity and ultimately to a Nietzchean nihilism. Stimulated by Heidegger, Yannaras turned to the Eastern theological tradition to find a way out of the nihilistic impasse Heidegger had identified. Yannaras saw the key lay in the distinction between "an *apophaticism of essence*, as exemplified by western scholasticism, and an *apophaticism of the person*, which characterizes the Christian thought of the Greek East."[1] Thus he began a personal study of the apophatic tradition in the Greek Fathers, focusing his attention on Dionysius the Areopagite, St Maximus the Confessor, and St John Climacus (John of the Ladder). "My first guide was Climacus—the guidance recorded in *Metaphysics of the Body*. Climacus referred me to the apophaticism of the Areopagite—and the fruit of *his* guidance was *Heidegger and the Areopagite*. The Areopagite was commented on by Maximus, and Maximus the Confessor fascinated me—the result: *Person and Eros*."[2]

But these works lay in the future. First came an important period of study at the University of Paris. Here he discovered the French medieval scholars Gilson and Chenu and, above all, the philosopher Jean-Paul Sartre. "To the challenges presented by Heidegger was now added the thrilling figure of Sartre: perhaps the most penetrating theological thinking of the century—theological like the negative of a photograph—and incomparably more metaphysical than the Western theologians."[3] What attracted him in particular was the way Sartre took philosophy out of the lecture room and into real life: "He was not content with systematic

---

[1]Christos Yannaras, *On the Absence and Unknowability of God: Heidegger and the Areopagite* (London: T&T Clark International, 2005), 29.

[2]Christos Yannaras, *Ta kath' eauton* [Personal experiences] (Athens: Ikaros, 2005), 50.

[3]Yannaras, *Ta kath' eauton*, 72. What Yannaras means is that Sartre's nihilism appeared to him as the negative of a photograph, as it were, of an empirical theology.

thinking, but laid bare his anguish in plays, novels, and free prose compositions."[4] It was in Paris, stimulated by Heidegger and Sartre, that Yannaras conceived of the project of confronting the ontological questions raised by them in the light of the ecclesial experience of the Greek Fathers of the Church, a project he knew would occupy him for the rest of his life. By the time he defended his doctoral thesis at the Sorbonne in May 1971, he had already published *Heidegger and the Areopagite*[5] and had prepared for publication the first version of *The Freedom of Morality*.[6]

Teaching Career

After being awarded a *doctorat ès lettres* for a thesis on the metaphysics of the body, Yannaras taught in Paris for two years (1971–73) as visiting professor both at the Institut de Saint Serge, the leading Orthodox seminary of the Russian emigration, and at the Institut Catholique, the Catholic university of Paris. He lectured on Byzantine philosophy at Saint Serge, and on the ontology of the person and ecclesial ethics at the Institut Catholique. During the same period (these were the years of the military dictatorship that governed Greece from 1967 to 1974), Yannaras submitted another thesis on a different topic to the University of Thessaloniki in order to prepare himself for eventual teaching in Greece. For this thesis, which was on the concept of the person, he was awarded a doctorate in theology with the highest distinction.

When he returned to Greece after the fall of the dictatorship, Yannaras taught first at a private school in Athens. Then, in 1977, he was invited to teach in the School of Theology of the University of Geneva, where he lectured on the ontology and ethics of

[4]Ibid.
[5]Published in English translation as *On the Absence and Unknowability of God: Heidegger and the Areopagite* (London: T&T Clark International, 2005).
[6]Published in English translation as *The Freedom of Morality* (Crestwood, NY: St Vladimir's Seminary Press, 1984).

the Greek ecclesial tradition. This was followed by three years (1979–82) at the School of Philosophy of the newly founded University of Crete, where he taught an introductory course on philosophy and philosophical ontology. Finally, in 1982, he was elected to the chair of philosophy at the School of International and European Studies of the Panteion University of Political and Social Sciences in Athens, where, for the next twenty years, until his retirement in 2002, he taught philosophical terminology and methodology, political philosophy, and cultural diplomacy.

A Metaphysical Adventure

Heidegger and Sartre had laid bare the nihilistic outcome of the Western metaphysical tradition, but they had not been able to propose an alternative. Heidegger had taken his starting point from Aristotle—what is it that unites all beings as Being?—and had investigated this fundamental question in the light of Husserl's phenomenology. Being is not some kind of supreme or ultimate being, as the Western tradition (based on the medieval principle of *adaequatio rei et intellectus*) had made it, but the "presentness" of beings to the human observer. To treat Being as a being, Heidegger claims, is to "onticize" it. According to the ontological (as opposed to the ontic) version of Being, we cannot know Being in itself; we can only know beings in the degree in which they are manifested. As Yannaras puts it, "the dynamic character of truth in Heidegger's philosophy is confined to the apprehension (*Verständnis*) of Being as temporality or absence, as the manifestation or the nothingness of a being. It has to do with a *mode of understanding* Being by the human subject, not with an interpretation of Being as Being."[7]

Yannaras's response in the light of the Greek (both pagan and Christian) philosophical tradition to the ontological questions

[7]Christos Yannaras, *The Schism in Philosophy: The Hellenic Perspective and Its Western Reversal* (Brookline, MA: Holy Cross Orthodox Press, 2015), 191.

raised by Heidegger finds its fullest expression in *Person and Eros*, first published under this title in 1974.[8] Here we have a detailed discussion, at a rigorous intellectual level, of what a personal "mode of existence" entails. The *prosōpon*, or person, is defined at the outset not in ontic terms, but as a reference and relation. To be a person is to be opposite someone or something. Persons are admittedly individuals, but not in the sense of subsisting in their completeness as discrete entities—they are individuals in the dynamic actualization of relationship. The mode of existence that is actualized in relation is "*ek-static*," which not only refers "to humanity's ability to 'stand outside' its natural identity [in accordance with the etymological meaning of *ek-static*], to wonder at its being . . . [but also] signifies self-transcendence from the naturally given capacity for intellectualization to the otherness of its personal actualization, from the self-evidentness of noetic-conscious conceptualization of objective conventionality and the naturally given common understanding of objective essences to universal existential relation."[9] This is what Yannaras, drawing on the Greek Fathers, means by *Eros*. Eros is "the loving impetus and movement of exodus from individualized existence in the realm of objects, for the sake of the actualization of *relation* in the highest sense."[10] We become persons through reaching out beyond ourselves to the other, a reaching out that finds it fulfillment as personal reference to the supremely Other.

[8]The publishing history of this work is complex. The first three parts were published in 1970 under the title *To ontologikon periechomenon tēs theologikēs ennoias tou prosōpou* [The ontological content of the theological concept of the person]. The second edition, with the title *To prosōpo kai ho erōs* [Person and eros], was published in 1974 by the journal *Deukalion*. The third edition was completed in six parts as *To prosōpo kai ho erōs. Theologiko dokimio ontologias* [Person and Eros. A theological essay on ontology] (Athens: Papazēsē, 1976). The English translation was made from the fourth edition, *To prosōpo kai ho erōs* (Athens: Domos, 1987): *Person and Eros* (Brookline, MA: Holy Cross Orthodox Press, 2007).

[9]Yannaras, *Person and Eros*, 20.
[10]Ibid.

Basilio Petrà has noted that in the 1987 edition of *To Prosōpo kai ho Erōs*, Yannaras makes a new move. He no longer limits himself to transposing patristic ontology into contemporary philosophical terms, but seeks to demonstrate the philosophical possibility of an ontology that is non-nihilistic, and therefore post-Heideggerian (and at the same time post-Kantian), capable of coexisting with what Yannaras terms "critical verification." "In other words, what has been elaborated earlier in the preceding works in reliance on the ontology of the Greek Fathers comes to be elaborated philosophically—in dialogue with Western philosophical thought—and through received philosophical categories, formally setting the Fathers to one side."[11]

Critical ontology is defined by Yannaras as "an ontology that is subject to critical verification, to empirical falsification."[12] This critical verification (or falsification) cannot be the result of a single individual's intellectual effort. Heraclitus had stated, "In so far as we share in common, we say what is true, but when we express our private thoughts, we say what is false."[13] For Yannaras this remains a permanently valid principle. What is true can be shared empirically; what is false cannot be shared empirically. The criterion of the communal verification of knowledge leads to an understanding of reality as relational: "whatever *is* becomes apparent only with reference to the person, is disclosed only within the terms of the *relation* which reveals the otherness of the person."[14] Thus the investigation of Being no longer concerns Being-in-itself, as an intellectual conception or as

---

[11]Basilio Petrà, *Christos Yannaras* (Brescia, Italy: Morcelliana, 2015), 74–75.

[12]Christos Yannaras, *To rhēto kai to arrhēto. Ta glōssika oria realismou tēs metaphysikēs* [What can be said and what cannot be said. The linguistic limits of the realism of metaphysics], 2nd ed. (Athens: Ikaros, 2008), 9. The principle of falsification comes from Karl Popper.

[13]Hermann Diels and Walther Kranz, *Fragmente der Vorsokratiker*, 6th ed., vol. 1 [Berlin: Wiedmannsche, 1952], 148, 28–29.

[14]Yannaras, *Person and Eros*, 19.

undetermined revelation and temporal disclosure, but Being as a *mode of existence.*[15]

In the second stage of his metaphysical inquiries, Yannaras enters into dialogue with several modern thinkers (both earlier and later than Heidegger), the most significant being Wittgenstein and Lacan. In *To rhēto kai to arrhēto* ("What can be said and what cannot be said"), which draws its title from the final proposition of Wittgenstein's *Tractatus Logico-Philosophicus*, Yannaras seeks "criteria for distinguishing the real from the illusory character of the experience of *relation* (of knowledge which is shared and communally attained) in its given interconnectedness with language (and its objective function)."[16] The field of his inquiry in this book is "the language of the references to the possibility of *human existence even after death*," for "every ontological hermeneutics walks a tightrope between nihilistic agnosticism and hope in life after death."[17] Wittgenstein's statement that the usage of a word in a language is that which constitutes its sense is the springboard for Yannaras's discussion of what meaning we can give to human existence after death. But he takes issue with Wittgenstein over the priority that must be accorded to experiential truth: "What even Wittgenstein does not suspect is that the greater (and principal) event of knowledge is the experiential immediacy of *relation*—the lesser (and derivative) one is the function of thought and language."[18] Wittgenstein's critique of the limitations of language, together with his distinction between *saying* and *showing*, are of immense value in highlighting the gnoseological origins of the modern impasse with regard to metaphysics. But despite his claim that the aim of philosophy is "to show the fly the way out of the fly-bottle,"[19] Wittgenstein does

[15]Ibid.
[16]Yannaras, *To rhēto kai to arrhēto*, 10.
[17]Ibid., 11.
[18]Ibid., 253.
[19]Ludwig Wittgenstein, *Philosophical Investigations*, G. E. M. Anscombe, trans. (Oxford: Blackwell, 1953), 309.

not arrive at showing the way out himself.[20] What is needed for this, in Yannaras's view, is an ontology of *relation*.

In his articulation of an ontology of relation, Yannaras finds valuable support in the writings of the psychoanalyst Jacques Lacan, especially his *Le Séminaire, Livre XI*, where Yannaras finds a key insight that he often quotes: "The subject is born in the measure in which the signifier is manifested in the field of the Other—the subject *in initio* begins in the place of the Other."[21] "If the subject originates in the Other's space," says Yannaras, "we may then make a fundamental distinction between the meanings of the terms *subject* and *biological individual*. The biological individual has an existential autonomy; it may be defined in itself. The subject not so; it may be defined only in relation to the space of the Other, in relation to the signifier's emergence in the Other's field."[22] Such emergence implies a distance separating us from the Other, a distance that Yannaras says we experience "as a life-giving desire for its transcendence . . . a desire for *life-as-relation*."[23] Moreover, "if the *birth* of the rational subject is not the result of biological necessity, why should its *death* be so? Why should the death of the rational subject not be the denial or rejection (not bound to biological necessity) of the life-giving reference of desire to the Other, of relation with the Other?"[24] There are no definitive answers. "The question of whether the 'Other' of our existential reference is the real (empirically accessible) second term of the fact of relation—and not a projection of desire or a compensation

[20]For Wittgenstein, ultimately "thought and language are the only possibility for a knowledge that is verifiable and communicable, because the *grammar* of language is the unique mirror of reality" (Yannaras, *To rhēto kai to arrhēto*, 255).

[21]Jacques Lacan, *Le Séminaire, Livre XI : Les quatre concepts fondamentaux de la psychanalyse* (Paris: Seuil, 1973), 180–81.

[22]Christos Yannaras, *Postmodern Metaphysics* (Brookline, MA: Holy Cross Orthodox Press, 2004), 163.

[23]Christos Yannaras, *Relational Ontology* (Brookline, MA: Holy Cross Orthodox Press, 2011), 115.

[24]Ibid., 117.

for insecurity—is . . . always a personal adventure of verification without any *a priori* guarantee of certainty."[25]

The Theological Dimension

The strict separation of philosophy from theology is a Western phenomenon with its roots in the different disciplines, or schools, of the medieval universities. Yannaras's metaphysical adventure, with its emphasis on a critical ontology and the priority of a personal mode of existence, had from the outset a theological dimension. God is not "a being," the ultimate in a series of beings. Nor is God bound to be simply what his essence defines him to be. The ancient philosophical view of God as subject to ontological necessity was overturned by the central point of the Christian gospel, the incarnation of God. If it is true that God can also exist as a human being without ceasing to be God, "then the existence of God is demonstrated to be free from logical prescriptions of essence or nature." And if God is existentially free from every necessity of mode of existence, "then there is a logical space for the 'grace' (the gift of being) that God can bestow on humanity with a view to humanity's sharing itself in the mode of freedom from the necessities of its essence or nature—namely, the necessities of decay, of death—limitations that accompany the nature of created being."[26]

When the Christian Gospel says that "God is love" (1 Jn 4.8), it is not referring to a divine attribute, an aspect of divine behavior. Although the being of God lies outside our epistemic capabilities (Yannaras takes an apophatic position on the knowledge of God), we can say that, in this context, love functions as a definition signifying the reality of divine being. The corresponding definition of a human being, setting aside any activities or behaviors, is that of "nature with accidents." If God as love is characterized by a

[25]Ibid., 119.
[26]Ibid., 50–51.

free disposition toward relation and self-offering, humanity as a nature with individuating accidents is characterized by subjection to necessity, but with a certain margin of freedom that is realized as relation. Our fulfillment as human beings lies in our developing this aspect of relation, that is to say, in ascending from the finite mode of nature, which is largely bound by necessity, to a mode of existence characterized by self-transcending referentiality, or love.

The narrative of the fall in the book of Genesis conveys these truths in symbolic form. What it presents is humanity's initial exercise of freedom through rejecting a personal relationship with God and choosing instead natural autonomy and self-sufficiency. Yannaras observes that this pseudo-divine autonomy (the serpent's promise of Gen 3.5, "You will be like God, knowing good and evil") is "an 'existential lie,' a fictitious possibility of life," because we can transcend the mortality of our nature only insofar as we realize the personal mode of existence that belongs to God alone.[27] That personal mode of existence partakes of communion and unity, whereas the fall, perpetuated in each generation, results in human nature being fragmented into a ruthless mass of individual wills that struggle competitively to maintain their natural self-sufficiency. To overcome the fall and attain the divine likeness, one must become a new creation in Christ. "In the person of Christ, human nature *subsists* as a personal hypostasis of communion with the divinity."[28] To begin to participate in this divinized humanity, this new mode of existence, we need simply to assent to Christ's love, to reject our self-sufficiency and simply desire to love and be loved. All that this preliminary step requires is the cooperation of our freedom.

After this first step we need to be grafted into the body of Christ through baptism and participation in the ecclesial life of

[27]Yannaras, *Freedom of Morality*, 30.
[28]Ibid., 52.

the Church. Such engrafting entails a transformation of our being through the liturgical sharing of Christ's body and blood: "The realization, manifestation, definition and essence of the Church is the eucharist, where the members of Christ come together and form His body: it is the unifying potential for a communion of persons within an undivided, new nature."[29] This draws on the eucharistic ecclesiology associated particularly with Metropolitan John Zizioulas, but Yannaras goes beyond Zizioulas in his careful working out of the ascetic dimension that must necessarily accompany the eucharistic. Asceticism is not obedience to an external law for the sake of the believer's justification as an individual. Rather, it is "the endeavour which confirms man's freedom and his decision to reject the rebellion of his individual will and to imitate the obedience of the second Adam."[30] Our imitation of Christ's obedience results in our embracing the Law in its true biblical sense: "The Law is a manifestation of God, a gift of grace—it is not juridical legislation serving a social purpose. It is a *call* to the people of Israel to receive and mediate the name of God, to be manifest as the 'radiance' of that truth which is God Himself."[31] And it is this manifestation of God that constitutes our recovery of the divine likeness.

It is for this reason that morality is not simply "conformity to an authoritative or conventional code of law," for this would be an escape from responsibility for oneself; it would be the adoption of a respectable alibi or ideological mask that enables people to ignore the existential questions that confront them.[32] Morality is rooted in human freedom and encompasses the whole trajectory of salvation: "What we call the morality or ethos of a man is the way he relates to the existential adventure of his freedom: morality manifests what man *is* in principle as an image of God—as a

[29]Ibid., 81.
[30]Ibid., 53.
[31]Ibid., 54–55.
[32]Ibid., 15.

person—and also what he *becomes* through the adventure of his freedom—a being transformed, or 'in the likeness' of God."[33]

Journalism

Yannaras began to write for a broader public than the readers of his major philosophical and theological works in the early 1960s, when he edited the journals *Skapanē* and *Synoro*. It was the imposition of military dictatorship in Greece in 1967, however, that first drew him into writing for newspapers. He began with the center-left newspaper *To Bēma* ("The Tribune") and later moved to the moderately conservative *Hē Kathēmerinē* ("The Daily"). For many years he has written a weekly column in the Sunday edition of *Kathēmerinē*. These articles, in which Yannaras comments from an independent viewpoint on many of the challenging cultural and political issues that the Greeks have had to deal with over the last decades, have been collected and published from time to time in more permanent form. Together with his appearances on television, they have made him a well-known public figure in Greece.

It is impossible to offer here an adequate evaluation of the thirty-six volumes (so far) of Yannaras's collected newspaper columns. But something needs to be said because, although none of these volumes has been translated into English, they represent an important dimension of his work. The first volume in this category,[34] *Hē krisē tēs prophēteias* ("The crisis of prophecy"), was first published in 1964 and is still in print in its fourth

[33]Ibid., 29.
[34]Yannaras divides his *oeuvre* into four categories: *Ta Philosophika* ("Philosophical works"), *Technēmata* ("Artifacts," i.e., literary works), *Ta Theologika* ("Theological works"), and *Chronographiai* ("Chronicles," i.e., articles commenting on topical issues in newspapers and journals). To these Basilio Petrà has added a fifth category, *Leitourgika* ("Liturgical texts"), to include the liturgical services in contemporary Greek that Yannaras first published anonymously (Petrà, *Christos Yannaras*, 161, 168).

edition.[35] Here in a series of short essays is a brilliant analysis of the critical state of Orthodox Christianity in Greece in the mid-twentieth century: its passivity in the face of rapid social and cultural change, its lack of a prophetic voice, its reliance on a theology of repetition. Yannaras compares this unfavorably with the theological ferment taking place at that time in the West in the wake of the Second Vatican Council. But his own work, as it happened, became a turning point of comparable significance for Greek theology. In introducing the third edition of 1981, the then publishers, Domos, declared, "If with the religious organizations and the academic style of theology confusion concerning the presuppositions and criteria of ecclesial experience and witness reach their peak, with *The Crisis of Prophecy* a language begins to be articulated which will express an initially weak but progressively stronger resistance to alienation."[36] Indeed, many of the themes that would be developed later in Yannaras's philosophical and theological works made their first appearance in these essays: the prophetic role of Dostoyevsky, the distinction between Christianity that is an act of faith/trust and Christianity that has been turned into a reassuring "religion," the "heresy" of the West (an exaggerated reliance on rational certainty as a presupposition of worldly power),[37] and the "heresy" of Orthodoxy (a spiritual smugness and self-sufficiency instead of the "right glory" [*orthē doxa*] that should be given to God).[38]

Yannaras has often been criticized for his "structural anti-Westernism." Certainly, "the West" is identified as the source of much that is lamentable in contemporary Orthodoxy. But it is

---

[35]Christos Yannaras, *Hē krisē tēs prophēteias* (Athens: Ikaros, 2010).

[36]Ibid., 9. It may be mentioned that *language* is used here also in the literal sense. Until the 1960s theological works had always been written in *katharevousa*, a stilted, archaizing version of Greek that was de rigueur in the universities. Yannaras was the first to conduct theological discussions in *dēmotikē*, the evolved language of the Greek people.

[37]Ibid., 89.

[38]Ibid., 90–97.

not simply a case of "us" against "them." "The West" stands for modernity's rationalism and utilitarianism, an outlook that has perverted the meaning of Christianity worldwide. Commenting on Yannaras's mature views (as expressed forty years later in *Enantia stē thrēskeia* ["Against religion"]), Basilio Petrà emphasizes that Yannaras has grafted the West-East dualism "onto a dualism that is broader and more radical: the dualism between *thrēskeiopoiēsē* [religionization] and ecclesial event, or rather, between *thrēskeia* [religion] and ecclesial event."[39] In Petrà's considered judgment,

> the term *West* in Yannaras's current thinking has a more general meaning that signifies the Christian's surrender to the temptation to transform the gospel message into a natural religion instead of assuming the natural religious need and transforming it in the eucharistic experience, in the ecclesial mode of existence. This temptation has found in the historical West a profound success of its own, but it is fully active everywhere and in all periods, not excluding the Orthodox Churches.[40]

Like many prophets, Yannaras is pessimistic about the future. A celebrated column published in *To Bēma* in July 1986 and entitled "Finis Graeciae"[41] begins with the scene of a madman in the streets of Athens shouting, "I am searching for Greece! Where is Greece? We have killed her, you and I. We are her murderers." Never mind, says Yannaras, that the madman has leaped out of the pages of Nietzsche, for he utters profound truths. Tradition,

---

[39]Petrà, *Christos Yannaras*, 120. See also Petrà, "Christos Yannaras and the Idea of 'Dysis,'" in *Orthodox Constructions of the West*, ed. George E. Demacopoulos and Aristotle Papanikolaou (New York: Fordham University Press, 2013), 161–80.

[40]Petrà, *Christos Yannaras*, 121–22.

[41]"Finis Graeciae" also provides the title for the volume of collected journalism of 1985–90 in which the article appears: Christos Yannaras, *Finis Graeciae* (Thessalonica: Ianos, 2014), 25–30.

cultural identity, and historical memory have all been destroyed by "luminaries" put into power by the Greek people. Yet the people, wrapped in the mantle of rampant consumerism, are oblivious to this: "The words of the madman touch us only externally, like winter cold."[42] The only meaning of life is derived from the laws of the market. Yannaras's apocalyptic image of people fighting for supplies in the supermarkets in the midst of a collapsing economy had become a reality by the time the article was republished in 2014, confirming his predictions of the consequences of an irresponsible, materialistic individualism.

Reception in Greece and Abroad

Yannaras's central role in the "renaissance" of Greek theology in the 1960s is widely recognized. In Greece his influence is indisputable. Even a scholar as critical of Yannaras's "Hellenocentrism" and "cultural understanding of Orthodoxy" as Pantelis Kalaitzidis acknowledges that he was "the first among us who formulated a clear and dynamic proposition for the dialogue of Orthodoxy with the challenges of the contemporary world, and moreover it was he who in the early days, so far as Greece was concerned—the 1960s—demonstrated the provincialism of ethnocentric ecclesiastical discourse and the broad range of ecumenical Orthodoxy."[43] Today much of the theological work conducted in Greece is in response to the challenges laid down by Yannaras.[44]

[42]Ibid., 26.

[43]Pantelis Kailaitzidis, "Hē anakalypsē tēs Hellēnikotētas kai ho theologikos antidytikismos" [The discovery of Hellenicity and theological antiwesternism], in *Anataraxeis stē metapolemikē theologia. Hē "theologia tou '60"* [The shake-up in postwar theology: The "theology of the 1960s"], ed. P. Kalaitzidis, Th. N. Papathanasiou, and Th. Ampatzidis, 512–13 (Athens: Indiktos, 2009).

[44]"It is no exaggeration," says Basilio Petrà, "that one can easily distinguish between pre-Yannaras and post-Yannaras theology in Greece, between theology as an academic discipline and theology as a passion for the fullness of life, for victory over death" (Petrà, *Christos Yannaras*, 7).

In Western Europe and North America, Yannaras has attracted scholarly attention from his very first publications. In 1972 Rowan Williams, then a young postdoctoral-research student, published a substantial essay on Yannaras's University of Thessaloniki thesis, welcoming it as "one of the most important theological studies to come from the Orthodox world in recent years."[45] By 1984 Bishop Kallistos of Diokleia was describing Yannaras as "widely regarded as the most creative prophetic religious thinker at work in Greece today."[46] In 2005 Andrew Louth pronounced Yannaras "without doubt the most important living Greek Orthodox theologian."[47] And in 2015 Basilio Petrà, the West's best expert on Yannaras, confirmed his continuing significance, calling him "one of the most important Orthodox thinkers of the second half of the twentieth century and the beginning of the present millennium."[48]

The serious engagement with Yannaras's philosophical work that began with Rowan Williams has continued with a significant number of articles,[49] culminating in 2015 in the first book-length

---

[45]R. D. Williams, "The Theology of Personhood: A Study of the Thought of Christos Yannaras," *Sobornost* 6 (1972): 415–30.

[46]Foreword to Yannaras, *Freedom of Morality*, 9.

[47]Introduction to Yannaras, *On the Absence and Unknowability of God*, 1.

[48]Petrà, *Christos Yannaras*, 7.

[49]Articles on Yannaras's philosophical work include all the contributions to D. Angelis et al., *Chrēstos Giannaras* (Athens: Manifesto, 2015); J. Cole, "Personhood in the digital age: the ethical use of new information technologies," *St Mark's Review* 233 (2015): 60–73; N. Depraz, "Das Individuum als Beziehungswesen. Die Marxinterpretation Michel Henrys im Vergleich mit F. J. Varela und Ch. Yannaras," in *Metaphysik des Individuums. Die Marxinterpretation Michel Henrys und ihr Aktualität*, ed. E. Angehrn and J. Scheidegger, 127–49 (Freiburg im Breisgau, Germany: Karl Halber, 2011); S. Mitralexis, "Person, Eros, Critical Ontology: An Attempt to Recapitulate Christos Yannaras' Philosophy," *Sobornost* 34.1 (2012): 33–40; I. Papagiannopoulos, "Re-appraising the Subject and the Social in Western Philosophy and in Contemporary Orthodox Thought," *Studies in East European Thought* 58.4 (2006): 299–330; D. Payne, "The 'Relational Ontology' of Christos Yannaras: The Hesychastic Influence on the Understanding of the Person in the Thought of Christos Yannaras," online at *https://www.academia.edu/1479462*; B. Petrà, "Personalist

Introduction

study in a Western language, by Basilio Petrà.⁵⁰ The person-centered, critical ontology that Yannaras proposes has also been tested in a number of doctoral theses but has not, so far, been falsified.⁵¹ As already noted, his theology is not easily separable from his philosophy, but this too has been discussed at a high level.⁵² Moreover, Christianity for Yannaras has profound social

Thought in Greece in the Twentieth Century: a First Tentative Synthesis," *The Greek Orthodox Theological Review* 50.1–4 (2005): 2–48; K. Stoeckl, "Post-secular Subjectivity in Western Philosophy and Eastern Orthodox Thought," in *Philosophical Theology and the Christian Traditions: Russian and Western Perspectives*, ed. D. Bradshaw, 187–97 (Washington, DC: The Council for Research in Values in Philosophy, 2012); and M. Sumares, "Signifying the Mystical as Struggle: Yannaras' Orthodox Refiguring of the Philosophy of Language," *Annals of the University of Bucharest*, Philosophy Series 63.1 (2014): 3–15.

⁵⁰This is his *Christos Yannaras*, published in Italian by Editrice Morcelliana of Brescia, Italy, which I have frequently cited. An English translation is forthcoming from Holy Cross Orthodox Press of Brookline, Massachusetts. In the same year (2015), the first book-length study of Yannaras was published in Greek: Angelis et al., *Chrēstos Giannaras*.

⁵¹Doctoral theses on Yannaras's philosophical thought include G. Ghio, "La deliberazione vitale come origine ultima della certezza applicata a Dio. Indagine sugli elementi d'ignoranza presenti nella certezza" (Pontificia Università Gregoriana, 2004), on Yannaras's gnoseology; E. Grigoropoulou, "The Early Development of the Thought of Christos Yannaras" (University of Durham, 2008); D. Gnau, "Person werden. Theologische anthropologie im Werk der Gegenwärtigen orthodoxen Theologen Panagiotis Nellas, Christos Yannaras und Ioannis Zizioulas" (Albert-Ludwigs-Universität, 2005), on Yannaras's anthropology; S. Mitralexis, "Ever-moving repose: The Notion of Time in Maximus the Confessor's Philosophy through the Perspective of a Relational Ontology" (Freie Universität, 2014); and A. Panagiotopoulos, "Physē kai prosōpo kata ton Chrēsto Giannara" (Aristotelian University of Thessaloniki, 2011), on Yannaras's personalism.

⁵²Doctoral theses on Yannaras's theology include Grigoropoulou's 2008 Durham University thesis (see the previous note); P. Kalaitzidis, "Hellēnikotēta kai Antidytikismos stē 'Theologia tou '60'" (Aristotelian University of Thessaloniki, 2008), on Yannaras's neo-Orthodoxy; and A. Polychronidis, "Hoi theologikes syntetagmenes tōn neuroepistēmōn. Paradeigmatikes anaphores ston John Eccles kai ston Chrēsto Giannara" (Aristotelian University of Thessaloniki, 2010), on Yannaras's theological use of evidence from the neurosciences. Articles and book chapters include D. Angelis, "Gia to *Enantia stē thrēskeia*," in idem et al., *Chrēstos Giannaras*, 73–77 (Athens: Manifesto, 2015), on Yannaras's book *Against Religion*; N. Loudovikos, "Ho erōs

and political consequences that have provided much of the subject matter of his journalism. As one of the more contested aspects of Yannaras's thought, it has not escaped scholarly attention.[53] Finally, as a philosopher, theologian, and political thinker, Yannaras has been honored with several honorary doctorates on both sides of the Atlantic.

One of the most remarkable things about Yannaras as a philosopher and theologian is how rapidly his stature has grown in the twenty-first century.[54] For a thinker who made his reputation

hōs hodos theologias kai eleutherias. Hē erotikē amphilogia tou Chrēsou Giannara," in idem, *Hoi tromoi tou prosōpou kai to basana tou erōta. Kritikoi stochasmoi gia mia mataneōterikēntheologikē ontologia*, 67–111 (Athens: Harmos, 2009), on the role of eros in Yannaras's theology; A. Louth, "Some recent works by Christos Yannaras in Translation," *Modern Theology* 25 (2009): 329–40; A. Nichols, "Christos Yannaras and Theological Ethics," in idem, *Light from the East: Authors and Themes in Orthodox Theology*, 181–93 (London: Sheed & Ward, 1995); A. Papanikolaou, "Personhood and its Exponents in Twentieth-Century Orthodox Theology," in *The Cambridge Companion to Orthodox Christian Theology*, ed. M. Cunningham and E. Theokritoff, 232–45 (Cambridge: Cambridge University Press, 2008); B. Petrà, " 'Communio' ecclesiale e genesi del soggetto morale," in *Quale dimora per agire. Dimensioni ecclesiologiche della morale*, ed. L. Melina and P. Zanor, 73–97 (Rome: PUL-Mursia, 2000); idem, "Ecclesialità ed etica Cristiana. Annotazioni sul pensiero di Ch. Yannaras e Y. Zizioulas," *Nicolaus* 30.1–2 (2003): 203–17; N. Russell, "Christos Yannaras (1935–) and Panayiotis Nellas (1936–1986)—Transcending Created Finitude," in A Companion on Recent Theological Movements, vol. 2, *Creation and Salvation*, ed. E. Conradie, 51–55 (Berlin: LIT Verlag, 2012); M. Sumares, "Apofatismo e estatuto ontológico da Igreja. O contributo de Christos Yannaras para a recuperação da racionalidade remanescente da Ortodoxia," *Communio: Revista Internacional Católica* 32.4 (2016): 419–32; R. Swinburne, "A Response to Christos Yannaras' *Against Religion*," *Oxbridge Philokalic Review* 2 (2013): 54–60; and N. Tănase, "Otherness and Apophaticism. Yannaras' Discourse of 'Personhood' and the Apophatic Theognosia," *Philotheos* 14 (2014): 254–67.
    [53]See especially D. P. Payne, *The Revival of Political Hesychasm in Contemporary Orthodoxy: The Political Hesychasm of John Romanides and Christos Yannaras* (Lanham, MD: Lexington Books, 2011); K. Stoeckl, "Contemporary Orthodox Discourses on Human Rights: the Standpoint of Christos Yannaras in a Political Philosophical Perspective," in *Orthodox Christianity and Human Rights*, ed. E. van der Zweerde and A. Brüning, 185–99 (Leuven: Peeters, 2012).
    [54]Of all the books, articles, and doctoral theses listed in notes 49–53, only one

in the 1960s, this is interesting. I would suggest the following reasons for it: First, although Yannaras would not classify himself as an "existentialist," his philosophical work draws on a continental personalist and existentialist tradition that has been out of fashion for some decades but has recently been brought into dialogue again with contemporary philosophical concerns. Second, Yannaras's prophetic voice has not become dated, nor, since retiring from his chair at the Panteion, has he ceased to write and publish works challenging many received opinions. Third, his ecumenical vision of Orthodoxy is all the more topical today in view of the problems caused by the nationalistic divisions in the Orthodox world, as reflected in competing ecclesiastical jurisdictions. Last, he has the ability to write in an accessible style without loss of intellectual rigor, which has gained him a growing readership for his works in translation. Most of the works available in a Western language before the end of the twentieth century were in French or Italian.[55] In the last decade, however, English has led the

was published in the last century. For a full bibliography, including earlier studies, see Petrà, *Christos Yannaras*, 172–79.

[55]Unsurprisingly, in view of Yannaras's teaching in Paris and Geneva, the first translations were into French: *De l'absence et de l'inconnaissance de Dieu* [*Hē theologia tēs apousias kai tēs agnōsias tou Theou*] (Paris: Éditions du Cerf, 1971); *La liberté de la morale* [*Hē eleutheria tou ēthous*] (Geneva: Labor et Fides, 1983); *Philosophie sans rupture* [*Schediasma eisagōgēs stē philosophia*] (Geneva: Labor et Fides, 1984); *La foi vivante de l'Église* [*Alphabētari tēs pistēs*] (Paris: Éditions du Cerf, 1989); *Vérité et unité de l'Église* [*Alētheia kai henotēta tēs ekklēsias*] (Grez-Doiceau, Belgium: Éditions Axios); and *Variations sur le Cantique des Cantiques* [*Scholio sto Asma Asmatōn*] (Paris: Desclée de Brouwer, 1992). Italian interest in Yannaras has always been strong, with seven books translated in the twentieth century (some from the French): *Ignoranza e conoscenza di Dio* [*Hē theologia tēs apousias kai tēs agnōsias tou Theou*] (Milan: Jaca Book, 1971); *La morale della libertà* [*Hē eleutheria tou ēthous*] (Milan: Jaca Book, 1973); *La libertà dell'ethos* [*Hē eleutheria tou ēthous*] (Bologna: EDB, 1984); *Variazioni sul Cantico dei Cantici* [*Scholio sto Asma Asmatōn*] (Cernusco sul Naviglio: CENS-Interlogos, 1992); *La fede dell'esperanza ecclesiale* [*Alphabētari tēs pistēs*] (Brescia: Queriniana, 1993); *Heidegger e Dionigi Areopagita, assenza e ignoranza di Dio* [*Heidegger kai Areopagitēs ē peri apousias kai agnōsias tou Theou*] (Rome: Città Nuova, 1995); and *Verità e unità della chiesa*

field,[56] with works also appearing in Italian[57] and in several Eastern European languages, notably Romanian, Russian, Serbian, and Ukrainian.[58] Yannaras's influence internationally is probably greater today—certainly in the English-speaking world—than at any time hitherto.

[Alētheia kai henotēta tēs Ekklēsias] (Sotto il Monte and Schio: Servitium editrice-Interlogos, 1995). In the same period only two books were translated into English: *The Freedom of Morality* [Hē eleutheria tou ēthous] (Crestwood, NY: St Vladimir's Seminary Press, 1984); and *Elements of Faith* [Alphabētari tēs pistēs] (Edinburgh: T&T Clark, 1991). There has only been one German translation: *Person und Eros* [To prosōpo kai ho erōs] (Göttingen: Vandenhoeck & Ruprecht, 1982).

[56]The English titles are: *Postmodern Metaphysics* [Meta-neōterikē Meta-physikē] (Brookline, MA: Holy Cross Orthodox Press, 2004); *On the Absence and Unknowability of God* [Heidegger kai Areopagitēs ē peri apousias kai agnōsias tou Theou] (London: T&T Clark International, 2005); *Variations on the Song of Songs* [Scholio sto Asma Asmatōn] (Brookline, MA: Holy Cross Orthodox Press, 2005); *Orthodoxy and the West* [Orthodoxia kai Dysē stē neōterē Hellada] (Brookline, MA: Holy Cross Orthodox Press, 2006); *Person and Eros* [To prosōpo kai ho erōs] (Brookline, MA: Holy Cross Orthodox Press, 2007); *Relational Ontology* [Ontologia tēs schesēs] (Brookline, MA: Holy Cross Orthodox Press, 2011); *The Meaning of Reality* [a selection of essays] (Los Angeles: Sebastian Press, 2011); *The Enigma of Evil* [To Enigma tou kakou] (Brookline, MA: Holy Cross Orthodox Press, 2012); *Against Religion* [Enantia stē thrēskeia] (Brookline, MA: Holy Cross Orthodox Press, 2013); and *The Schism in Philosophy* [Schediasma eisagōgēs stē philosophia] (Brookline, MA: Holy Cross Orthodox Press, 2015).

[57]The Italian titles (all translated by Basilio Petrà) are: *Ontologia della relazione* [Ontologia tēs schesēs] (Troina: Città aperta, 2010); *Contro la religione* [Enantia stē thrēskeia] (Magnano: Comunità di Bose, Qiqajon, 2012); *La libertà dell'ethos* [Hē eleutheria tou ēthous], rev. based on the Greek ed. of 2002 (Magnano: Comunità di Bose, Qiqajon, 2014).

[58]Bulgarian, Finnish, Polish, and Slovenian can also claim a single title each. The most widely translated work overall is *Heidegger kai Areopagitēs ē peri apousias kai agnōsias tou Theou.*

PART I

Formative Influences

Norman Russell: *It has been said that "every system of thought, be it theological or secular, is in essence the attempt of one individual to come to terms with their own life experience."*[1] *What would you say, Christos, is the "life experience" that has been most formative in the development of your own thinking?*

Christos Yannaras: A searching question, Norman. If I am in a position to judge objectively, my research throughout the whole of my life, up to the present, has been influenced chiefly by two factors: my experience during my childhood and youth of the pietistic "Zoe" movement with its Protestant character, and my timely encounter with the work of Martin Heidegger.

The Zoe Movement

During my years in the Zoe movement, I experienced in a direct manner something of the Western world—some elements of its religious tradition, which many people are unwilling to regard as the most representative but that Nietzsche, at least, would have claimed are the ones that have shaped Western culture. If you were to ask me to paint a picture of what it was like to grow up in an atmosphere of pietism, I would refer you to two cinematographic masterpieces: the Danish film *Babette's Feast*

---

[1] Oliver Davies, *God Within: The Mystical Tradition of Northern Europe* (New York: New City Press, 1988), 37.

by Gabriel Axel (1987) and the Swedish *Fanny and Alexander* by Ingmar Bergman (1982). The perverted privation of life and joy for the sake of a pious moralism in the first film and a frightful tyranny of religious authoritarianism in the second can be appreciated for their brilliant authenticity only by those who have themselves experienced a pietistic environment in whatever religious tradition.

So, in my religious education and experience, I am purely Western. The same may be said for my early theological training in the thoroughly Western-oriented Theological School of the University of Athens. But in my secular education and social upbringing too, I am a typical product of the (Athenian) middle class (of the capital of the modern Greek national state), which was formed and functions as a poor imitation of the Western model of life. Thus, when I judge the West and its culture, I am not judging something outside myself, some opposing culture. I am judging my own life, my outlook, the reflexes and habits that are part of my psychological makeup. And I am searching the historical past of the West proper for answers to the tragedy of the errors depicted by Axel and Bergman, or those proclaimed by Nietzsche. And I have experienced these errors personally, as many Europeans have, in my inner being.

NR: *What made you leave Zoe?*

CY: I left Zoe because of (mainly) three people who inoculated me at a certain point in time with a suspicion that proved very fruitful. A suspicion that the language I spoke, my mother tongue, and the worship in which I participated preserved, in spite of me, a vital difference from my own mode of life and my borrowed Western culture. That this difference had a specific historical beginning: the division of Christianity into its Western and Eastern forms. And that in spite of the fact that the culture of the West had swallowed up the Greco-Roman East centuries ago, remnants of the difference were still preserved in the popular ethos, in the tradition of folk art and in the practices of daily life, right down to the time of my grandfathers' birth.

The three people who inoculated me with these suspicions were a poet and literary critic, Zissimos Lorentzatos; a wise architect and painter, Dimitrios Pikionis; and an almost marginal cosmopolitan teacher with an astonishing philosophical and theological formation, Dimitris Koutroubis.[2] The first two helped me, without formally instructing me, to begin to appreciate what treasures of the "meaning" of life and existence were embodied in the folk tradition of my own country, like traces of an artless nobility at the opposite pole to Western utilitarianism, that baleful product of individualism. The third, Koutroubis, taught me by his Socratic charm how to draw from the texts of the Fathers not ideological crutches of objective "infallibility," but the witness of ecclesial experience and how to discern the relevance of this witness today.

With these as givens, the difference between the Greco-Roman world and the Latino-Germanic West was not simply a fascinating field of research for me. It was above all a need to find my bearings in the specific historical time and culture in which I happened to live, a need to find "meaning" in the fact of a schizoid identity: that I was baptized "Orthodox" and yet that my mode of life, my mode of thinking, feeling, and acting, had been formed historically by Roman Catholicism and Protestantism.

I suspected that the various attributed "meanings" that also differentiate *modes* of life or cultures may be identified as different attitudes toward the human body, that metaphysics should be judged on the level of material embodiedness. I wanted to write a dissertation with the paradoxical title "The Metaphysics of the Body," in which I would study the cultural difference between

---

[2]Biographical notes on these and other people mentioned in the course of the discussion may be found in the prosopography.

Orthodoxy and the West, if it exists, in perhaps the most austere text of the Orthodox ascetical tradition, *The Ladder* of John of Sinai.

I was a student in Germany. I began looking for books in the library of the university's Faculty of Philosophy (at Bonn) with a view to investigating the meaning of the word "metaphysics." During my search I came across Heidegger's *Introduction to Metaphysics*. It was the beginning of a revelation for me.

The Divine Liturgy

NR: *Heidegger's treatment of metaphysics is manifestly fundamental to your own approach. We shall return to him. But for the moment, I want to stay with your earlier experiences. As a child you were exposed to a strongly Russified version of the Liturgy, singing as you did in the polyphonic choir at the Royal Palace, and not just occasionally but frequently, especially throughout Great Week, for five years. What awakened in you an appreciation of the Byzantine liturgical tradition?*

CY: When I was a child, my whole religious upbringing was intensely Western. The form of the Russian Liturgy therefore appealed very much to me, and I fell in love with it. It envoked in me a sense of euphoria and elation, an emotional satisfaction—all the marks of an individualized religiosity. Besides, in most of the Athens churches at that time, the singing was European, i.e., polyphonic. During the years I spent in Paris, I encountered the Russian style of liturgical singing again in the Francophone parishes where I usually went to church (rarely in the Greek ones). Sometimes I recall it nostalgically for the memories it brings back to me, in spite of its musical poverty and tiresome monotony.

I discovered the so-called Byzantine liturgical chant when I returned to Greece and chose to attend a small church in the Plaka belonging to the exarchate of the Patriarchate of Jerusalem. The cantor there was a little old man, Theodoros Hatzitheodorou, an expert in "Byzantine" music, which he taught for several decades at the Athens Odeon. With a number of friends, I experienced many happy years at this church. There was no electric lighting, only candles and lamps. Consequently, there were no microphones either. Gradually a parish gathered round this church, a warm company of friends. Koutroubis often came, and sometimes Zissimos Lorentzatos. There were a lot of young people too, students in jeans and long hair, something you didn't see in other churches. In this atmosphere I began to understand that "something else" that is ecclesial chant, another form of expression, another language—with the aim that it should "pass over" to the communion of relations rather than serve the individualism of aesthetic pleasure and spiritual uplift.

Mount Athos

NR: *In the "Zoe" movement, as you say, Mount Athos was regarded simply as a refuge for dirty and ignorant old men. The only point of going there was to solicit subscriptions for the "Zoe" periodical. Tell me about your first visit to Mount Athos. After leaving "Zoe," did you ever consider a monastic vocation?*

CY: I visited the Holy Mountain for the first time in a group excursion organized by "Zoe," I think at the end of the 1950s. I do not remember much about it, only how very impressed I was by the monk Theokletos Dionysiatis. Ever since then, there has been a close bond between us. Later, under the influence of Zissimos (Lorentzatos), I was consumed by great curiosity (and perhaps also by the need to find some substitute for the "authority" that "Zoe" had provided for me) about the Holy Moutain. At any rate, I wanted to meet some "elders" at that time known to a relatively small circle, people with ecclesial rather than pietistic criteria. In this period I went to Paros to see Fr Philotheos

Zervakos at Longovarda. (I learned when I was there that this monastery had been endowed in the nineteenth century by ancestors of mine on my mother's side, named Vosyniotis, who originated from Tegea in Arcadia.) I traveled to Patmos to meet Fr Amphilochios Makris, with whom I also formed a friendship. I used to visit him regularly for a number of years. Zissimos introduced me to Fr Athanasios Hamakiotis, at Neratziotissa of Amarousios, and to the Elder Theodoulos at the little Monastery of St John in the castle of Koroni, and once we went together to a service at the little monastery of a certain Kyprianos, who later I think became an Old Calendarist bishop. I was searching. For some years I was close to Fr Paisios, who has become very well known today; to Fr Ephraim Katounakiotis; to Fr Ieronymos of Aegina; and also to Fr Porphyrios, who at the time was chaplain at the Athens Polytechnic.

On leaving "Zoe," I began going to the Holy Mountain, chiefly at Easter, when I came back to Greece from Germany or France. I had discovered a small monastery, the Hermitage of the Danielaioi in the Holy Mountain's "desert" at Katounakia (very near Karoulia, where ascetics live in caves). The superior of the Danielaioi was a striking little elder, the gentlest of men, called Fr Gerontios, who came from Aivali in Asia Minor. He loved me very much, and I in turn adored him. When I published *The Freedom of Morality* in 1970 and was immediately attacked by the cadres of the pietistic organizations with fearful slanders and insults (they felt threatened by this book, and not without reason), even my beloved Fr Gerontios turned against me. He wrote to me with much pain, but without any harshness, that I was not to visit their monastery again. In the meantime, Fr Vasileios (Gontikakis) and Fr Paisios had settled in the Monastery of Stavronikita. Henceforth, this monastery became my Athonite base.

This is how I would give an "objective" sketch of my relations with the Holy Mountain. The experiences that accompanied these relations belong to another story.

Germany

NR: *When you left Zoe, France would seem to have been the obvious choice for your further studies. Why did you choose Germany?*

CY: When I was leaving for Germany in 1964, Evangelos Papanoutsos, a teacher and philosopher who was very well known and respected in Greece, said to me, "I shall repeat to you the advice which Cavafy gave me when I was leaving Alexandria to go and study in Germany: 'Go to Germany to pursue a serious program of studies, and then afterward go to France and forget what you learned in Germany!'" Indeed, in those years, study in a German university, especially in the theoretical and human sciences, was regarded as a guarantee of academic seriousness, as evidence of an excellent training in methodical and organized academic work. France, in the common view, had other virtues: it was the country that gave priority to cultivating an artistic sensibility, to promoting research in the arts; it was the country of creative stimuli, of avant-garde initiatives, the society in which something new was constantly happening and offering fertile challenges.

These, of course, were superficial social clichés. I wanted to go to France for other reasons, primarily to get to know the Russian diaspora that had established itself there and its striking offspring, the Francophone Orthodox parishes. What was of supreme importance for me, however, was the need I felt to apply myself to serious university study and to the method of research—I was aware of how superficial and low-level my education had been in the Greek university system. Moreover (and very importantly), the scholarships provided by the (then) West German government were the best in Europe.

In hindsight, I believe that Germany was for me a real *statio*,[3] for it was there, quite "by chance," without seeking it out, that I encountered the work of Martin Heidegger. If this encounter had not taken place, the challenge of the *ontology of the person* would not have emerged in my life.

France

NR: *In Paris in the 1960s, you knew many of the second-generation Russian émigré theologians. Florovsky, Meyendorff, and Schmemann had, I think, already gone to New York. But you met Paul Evdokimov, and among those you knew well were Nicolas Lossky, Boris Bobrinskoy, Pierre Struve, Michel Evdokimov, and Olivier Clément. How did they regard you? What did you take back from these contacts?*

CY: In Paris, in the five years I spent there, I participated enthusiastically in the life of the Francophone Orthodox community. I lived my participation; I felt as if the Francophone Orthodox were my own family. I usually went to church at the "crypt" of the Russian cathedral in the rue Daru, where an astonishing doctor, Fr Pierre Struve, served the Liturgy. He worked all the week at the hospital and then on Sundays was the celebrant in the "crypt." The choir was led by Michel, the son of Paul Evdokimov, and the organizing "soul" of the parish was Nina, Paul's daughter and Michel's sister. Olivier Clément regularly attended the Liturgy there.

Sometimes I also liked to go to the Francophone parish of the rue Saint-Victor in the Latin Quarter. There the tone was set by the Lossky family: Nicolas, Vladimir's son, and his sisters, with

---

[3]*Statio*, a Latin expression for a stopping place or residence, was also a military term for a guard post or watch. Here it indicates a significant staging post on the march toward engagement with the ontology of the person.

their families. The celebrant was Fr Gabriel Henry, who worked in an insurance office. Regular churchgoers there included Leonid Ouspensky and his wife—I was very fond of them.

I formed a close bond with the Orthodox of Paris, with Olivier Clément, Fr Boris Bobrinskoy, Nicolas Lossky, Paul and Michel Evdokimov, and others less well known. I admired the liveliness of their parishes and the theological discourse that informed their sermons. I have written something about these experiences in my book *Ta kath' eauton*. I went to Paris so filled in advance with enthusiasm as a result of the books written by the Russians and Olivier Clément that I was slow to admit something that I constantly observed while living there: another kind of pietism, different from the one I had experienced in Zoe, but still with the same basic features. The first generation of Russian émigrés must have possessed a powerful strand of ecclesial realism in its theology. They had known the Church embodied on Russian soil as a "mode" of daily life. The second and third generations had been born in the West. They had completed their schooling in the West. They lived the daily life of Western people and obviously shared in their mentality. Their faith could not help having, for the most part, the character of "convictions"; their piety could not avoid the formalistic character of Western "deontology"; their understanding of *askēsis* could not escape the legalism of Western moralism. Moreover, the Russian popular tradition itself had as a dominant element an individualist sensibility, the individualism of a guilt-ridden conscience. In Russian worship a characteristic goal is the individual's sense of exaltation and elation, an almost voluptuous psychological tenderness.

This is a large and important topic that I have never ventured to broach in any of my books, nor, of course, can we analyze it here. Unfortunately, I was too late to get to know Vladimir Lossky. And I only met Fr Florovsky once, at a conference in England—his books give me no cause to discern even a trace of the religionized version of the ecclesial event. Of course, we are all frail human beings with many contradictions. That is why it is difficult to explain how a great theological figure like Fr Schmemann can leave behind—alongside his excellent book *For the Life of the World*—a *Journal* typically pietistic in its language and outlook.

It is a drama common to us all: the "mode" in which we exist, in which we lead our daily lives, is absolutely Western, and we try to ensure that our "convictions" and our conduct remain ecclesial—it is a really schizoid situation for us. In recent years Francophone Orthodoxy (*Fraternité Orthodoxe*) seems content to be regarded as a tradition of "spirituality" parallel to, but not asymptotic with, other corresponding "spiritualities"—for example, the Roman Catholic, which it regards as very close to it. The word "spirituality" has almost replaced the term "*ecclēsia*," or "Church." The sense has been lost that "Church" refers to the transition from the individualistic "mode" of existence to the imaging of the "mode" of the uncreated Trinity—not to atomic convictions and atomic conduct.

During the last part of my stay in France, my friends' attitude toward me changed very strikingly. They had marked me with the stigma of the "anti-Westener." I felt that they had put me in quarantine. The French translator of my book *To alphabētari tēs pistēs*[4] wrote a fiercely hostile critique of the book, castigating what he regarded as "anti-Western." I struggled to retain a basic degree of authorial dignity. At the last moment, without my knowledge, the title was altered, and a purely pietistic one was adopted: *La foi vivante de l'Eglise*—instead of *La foi de l'experience de l'Eglise*, which had been agreed in the contract.

---

[4]13th ed. (Athens: Domos, 2006), trans. into English as *Elements of Faith* (Edinburgh: T&T Clark, 1991).

PART II

Hermeneutic Principles

Being and Relation

NR: *You have criticized the Western tradition of metaphysics as a "science of being" relying on a priori methods and have proposed an alternative first philosophy based on the dynamics of relationship. But do you not have to have "something" before there can be a relation?*

CY: A presupposition of thinking philosophically (a real presupposition, not a methodological-intellectual a priori) is that there should be a subject of the act of thinking philosophically, a rational subject capable of philosophical thought. I must exist in order to be able to think philosophically.

The West's difference from the ecclesial Hellenic tradition lies in the following: The West makes *existing* different from *being related*, and takes *relation* as a property-capacity that characterizes only certain existents (a mark of recognition of rational beings), whereas ecclesial Hellenism recognizes existence as an event of active relations—it identifies *existence* with *relation*. The understanding that I personally draw from the testimony of ecclesial experience is that existing in itself constitutes an act of *relation*. I do not first exist and then subsequently come into relation; I exist *because* I am related.

In the case of the Causal Principle of existing and of existents, the language of ecclesial experience is clear. The Causal Principle is not an individual divinity, a being, in itself, "a being that is supremely divine, a genus held in the highest honor" (such as Zeus, Uranos, and Kronos). What comes first existentially and definitively is not the Godhead, with its threefold character following next as a property or mark of recognition. The Causal Principle of what exists is not that which it is because it is "God," but because it is the *Father*: he who constitutes existence as *relation* (that is, as the freedom of love), he who "begets" the Son and causes the Spirit to "proceed." His *being* is not Godhead; it is threefoldness, relation—"God is *love*."

The human subject corresponds to this. We do not first exist and then subsequently come into relation, but rather, we exist *because* we are related; our existence is the *hypostatic* (existentially real) realization of a response to a call-to-relation, to the summons by which the Cause of existence has called us from *non-being into being*. God's summons constitutes me as an existence, and the *mode* of my existence is the freedom to give substance to my yes or my no to a loving-erotic call-to-relation with my Creator; it is the freedom to realize my existence as a developing affirmation or denial of divine love for my "person."

Even if we examine human existence from the biological point of view, it is also an event of dynamic *relations*. Human beings do not exist if they do not breathe; if they are not nourished with food; and if they have no relationship with the materials that ensure clothing, tools, and shelter. A rational subject is not constituted by language (that is, by thought) except through a *relation* with its mother—Lacan has shown us that "the first signifier is manifested in the place of the Other (at the mother's breast)"; it is there, in relation, that language—that is to say, the rational subject—is brought to birth.

The theory of relativity, the uncertainty principle, and the study of the quantum field have also changed our perception of inanimate existences. We have perceived that the sensible universe, the macrocosm and the microcosm, is not a totality of given entities, but a totality of active relations. There is not "something" in the universe "before" the active event of the relations that constitute it.

If we distinguish *being* from *relation*, in the manner of the leading thinkers of the Western tradition (Augustine, Aquinas, Kant), the question inevitably arises: What is *being*? We ask about *being* as "some-thing," not as some kind of *how* (not as a *mode*). The impasse to which this "ontic" questioning of *being* leads us is brilliantly resolved by Heidegger: the question "*what* is *being*?" necessarily binds us either to a dogmatic a priori or to a (logically and empirically) consistent nihilism.

Martin Heidegger and His Influence

NR: *In several of your works, you have described how Heidegger opened your eyes to the bankruptcy of Western metaphysics, that is to say, of a tradition going back to the medieval Schoolmen that made God a being like other beings in the universe, only qualitatively far superior. Such a being, even though endowed with the superlative attributes of infinitude, omniscience, and omnipotence, proved vulnerable to advances in the positive sciences and to the philosophical nihilism of Nietzsche and ultimately Heidegger. One of the most perceptive students of your work, Basilio Petrà, has written, "One may justly say—in my opinion—that from 1966 onwards the comparison with Heidegger remains the explicit/implicit horizon of Yannaras's reflection in such a way that Heidegger's interpretation of the West becomes for him canonical or normative."[1] Would you agree with that? And how do you answer those of your critics who doubt whether you can adopt Heidegger's philosophical perspective without also taking on his nihilism?*

[1]Basilio Petrà, "Christos Yannaras and the Idea of 'Dysis,'" in *Orthodox Constructions of the West*, ed. George E. Demacopoulos and Aristotle Papanikolaou (New York: Fordham University Press, 2013), 168–69.

CY: No, I wouldn't agree with Petrà's remark. I have never sought in Heidegger any canonical or normative "authority" that would validate my critical stance with regard to the gnosiological and ontological choices or theories that have been cultivated in the West. In Heidegger I encountered a strikingly formulated proposition interpreting the "death of God" in the West, as proclaimed by Nietzsche. His interpretation showed that this real event was the inevitable result of an intellectualist gnosiology that isolated the ontological problem from any possible empirical verification. Heidegger was bold enough to pose the ontological question in a manner that rejected formal logical correctness as self-evident truth and attributed to "truth" the empirical character of "appearing" (of "coming to light") as the ancient Greeks did. He identifies as the "horizon" of *appearing* the exclusively human capacity for *consciousness of time*: the experience of existence as temporality. And with this as a starting point, he reformulates the ontological question as a multifaceted problem with a wonderfully consistent emphasis on the priority of the experiential (the experience of *existing*). He clearly ended up with a nihilistic ontology (with theories that nullified the idols of the "certainties" of intellectualism), but what concerns me is the methodological integrity of the way the problem is put, the completeness of the thematic analysis of the ontological question, not the reputed nihilism of the conclusions. I wanted to test, to investigate, whether the witness of ecclesial experience and its language (starting with the Christian literature of the first centuries of our era) contained any methodologically and empirically coherent answers to Heidegger's problematic.

NR: *Which you do at greatest length in* Person and Eros.

CY: *Person and Eros* does indeed owe a lot to Heidegger's thesis and analysis of the ontological question. But the Church fathers too owe the shaping of a great part of their problematic (and their language) to Aristotle, Plato, and Plotinus. Their adoption of questions and methods from them cannot be construed as necessarily the reception of any of their own conclusions and assumptions.

The assertion that *Person and Eros* attempts to "justify" patristic theology by the "use" of Heidegger appeared for the first time in 1977 (seven years after it was first published) in a study by John Zizioulas (now metropolitan of Pergamon and a member of the Academy of Athens) entitled *From Mask to Person*. It was in this text that Zizioulas first concerned himself with the ontological problem, and the methods of scholarly argument required that he should not ignore the only study on the *ontology of the person* that had appeared to date. He dedicated a footnote of some length to *Person and Eros* in order to condemn what he supposed to be the book's argument, none of which, however, was actually in the book. It was abundantly clear that Zizioulas had not read *Person and Eros*, or even any of Heidegger's works. He was acquainted only with certain of Lévinas's criticisms of Heideggerian ontology (in his *Totalité et Infini*), and perhaps the table of contents of *Person and Eros*.

This observation does not diminish the value and significance of *From Mask to Person*. It simply explains why the perception has prevailed in the West that *Person and Eros* attempts to "vindicate" the witness of the Fathers by recourse to the "authority" of Heidegger. The condemnatory footnote was translated (together with the study that contained it) into French in 1981 and into English in 1985, but *Person and Eros* only appeared in English in 2007.

NR: *Zizioulas's criticism is certainly severe, complaining as it does that although Heidegger's thought liberates ontology from absolute "ontism," it imports temporality into the idea of God, ontologizes death, and reduces truth to an outgrowth from oblivion. But is it fair to attribute a negative perception of your work in the*

West largely to his comments? Rowan Williams, John Saward, and Philip Sherrard, in reviews published in the 1970s, all express reservations about your use of Heidegger. This was at a time when there was widespread resistance in the English-speaking world to anything Heideggerian—one philosophical encyclopedia even claimed that "there are probably few philosophers to whose vogue Andersen's fairy tale, The Emperor's Clothes *is more applicable."[2] Nowadays the philosophical climate seems more favorable.*

CY: Let me dwell for a moment, if I may, on some words that I would not agree with. I would not describe Zizioulas's brief criticism of *Person and Eros* (in a footnote to a brief study of his) as "severe." I would simply say that it is irrelevant: it condemns theses and viewpoints (or makes conjectures) that have no basis in the book. I would therefore be so bold as to surmise that he wrote this note without having read either my own study or any of Heidegger's works.

Zizioulas acknowledges (as you say yourself in your comment) that Heidegger liberates ontology from absolute "ontism" and rationalism, even if not in fact from the concept of consciousness and of the subject. And he "defends" this assertion by referring to a passage in Lévinas, which runs, "*Being and Time* has perhaps maintained no more than a single thesis: that being is inseparable from the understanding of being (an understanding that functions/is conducted/flows as time); being is already a call to subjectivity."

But Lévinas's comment has nothing to do with the "ontism" or the rationalism from which Heidegger liberated ontology. Lévinas attributes to Heidegger the identification of *being* with the *understanding of being*, that is to say, that he escapes from the field of ontology to the field of epistemology, as Kant also

---

[2]J. O. Urmson, ed., *The Concise Encyclopaedia of Western Philosophy and Philosophers* (London: Hutchinson, 1960), 162.

does. Whether this assertion of Lévinas's is true or not is another problem. It has no relation to the "ontism" and rationalism that Zizioulas invokes.

Heidegger did indeed liberate the problem of ontology from getting bogged down in "ontism," but I fear that Zizioulas does not understand that noematic content of the term. Otherwise he would not have spoken of "absolute" ontism. There is neither relative nor absolute ontism; such a distinction has no logical place. Ontism is the sense of the verbal noun "being" (*einai*) as the present participle "being" (*ōn*). In other words, it is asking *what is it* (what is the something) that makes beings be? Heidegger transforms the problem in a radical way by asking not "What is the relation?" but "What is the *difference* between beings and being?"

Moreover, Zizioulas does not discern that Heidegger liberated ontology from intellectualism, not from rationalism. Rationalism is to reason correctly; it is the (empirically shared) rational correctness of expression. Intellectualism, on the other hand, has the sense of merely noetic apprehension (*cogito*) as the actual given of that which exists.

John Saward, on the other hand, in his review of the *Metaphysics of the Body*, expresses enthusiasm for "the connection between the Fathers and Heideggerian philosophy," and wonders only at the emphasis given to *Sein und Zeit* rather than to Heidegger's later works. Philip Sherrard's reservations had to do with identifications and differences concerning the semantic content of words encountered in both the Fathers and Heidegger—how the Fathers understand the concepts of nothingness, of being as *einai*, and of being as *ōn*; and how Heidegger understands them. He believes that "behind modern philosophical language lies a development of human thought unknown and alien to the Fathers." He wishes that a clarification of the two usages (by the Fathers and by Heidegger) of the same terminology had preceded *Person and*

Eros. But such a clarification, in my view, could not have been achieved simply by a word study, but only by a reformulation of the ontological question, as in *Person and Eros.* If this book has any significance in the history of philosophical enquiry into matters of ontology, it is precisely because it demonstrates that the language-terminology of the Fathers is closer to the intellectual and experiential content of Heidegger's language-terminology than it is to that of Aquinas or Hegel. And when I say "closer," I do not mean "ideological" correspondences (which Sherrard rightly fears), but common demands for the empirical exploration of the "sense" (or non-sense) of the real and the existent.

In Rowan Williams's review article (occupying fifteen pages in *Sobornost*; the fullest and most systematic review that has ever been written on any of my books), I do not recall any specific query or reservation about my use of Heidegger. What precisely do you have in mind?

NR: *Certainly, in his critique of* The Ontological Content of the Theological Concept of the Person, *the earliest version of* Person and Eros, *Williams is highly appreciative of the way you have attempted, as he puts it, a synthesis of the Greek patristic tradition and modern phenomenological thought, and he acknowledges the importance of the book. But he does wonder how necessary the "explicitly Heideggerian framework" is and suggests that there may be some parallel with the way Russian theologians in the late nineteenth and early twentieth centuries made use of Hegel.[3] The danger of a "Hellenic Slavophilism" seems to him a real one—or at least it did at the time of writing, nearly four decades ago. Perhaps this is no more than the reaction, as he suspects, of an Anglo-Saxon philosophical mind "to what appears to be Teutonic mystification."[4] I myself think that such fears are much*

[3]R. D. Williams, "The Theology of Personhood: A Study of the Thought of Christos Yannaras," *Sobornost* 6 (1972): 415–30.
[4]Ibid., 416.

exaggerated, and have more to do with Anglo-American attitudes to Heidegger than with the use you actually make of him.

CY: Perhaps I might make a general comment here. If I am not mistaken, in the field of philosophy (which is the heading under which the Greeks have always regarded theology as belonging) there are two *ways* of working: in today's terminology we speak of a literary-historical approach to the "sources" and of their "systematic" use.

In the former case, what is of prime importance to students is that they should protect the text from misunderstandings and misinterpretations, that they should give us a valid interpretation of the argument set out by the author. The validity of the interpretation is dependent on the student's linguistic endowment and critical capacity (so as to identify criteria of interpretation both within the text itself and also in the contingent-historical influences to which the author has been subject).

In the latter case, what interests the student is a problem, not a text. The student seeks direct or indirect responses in texts from a variety of different authors (who do not necessarily agree with each other). The student has a duty not to force or distort the texts in order to construct a desired response to the problem under consideration, but it is entirely legitimate for him or her to be "inspired" by a text, that is to say, to discern in a particular formulation some extension of meaning or proof from experience that the author himself or herself was perhaps not aware of.

It is a serious error to confuse these two methods, the literary-historical and the synthetic-systematic, an error that creates a lack of understanding. Such confusion prevents us from attaining the goal of either of these methods. Personally, in what I have written myself, I have been helped in a vital way by the works of Heidegger, Maximus the Confessor, Wittgenstein, and Isaac the Syrian. I do not pretend to be an authoritative interpreter of Heidegger, or Maximus, or Wittgenstein, or Isaac. The craft I have practiced and still practice is the systematic-synthetic variety, and if I have any speciality, it is in problems, not in the authoritative interpretation of authors' texts.

When you pursue synthetic-systematic studies, you are judged both on whether you are possibly betraying the borrowings you have made from other writers, and also on the coherence and exactitude of your systematic synthesis. It is a presupposition for both aspects of this work, and also for their critical evaluation, that one should have a satisfactory knowledge both of the entire oeuvre of the author one is using and also of the requirements of methodological coherence in the synthesis that is being attempted. Unfortunately, in the case of the *ontology of the person*, many have supposed that this is all to do with kerygmatic theology. As a result, they think they can judge the specialized scholarly work and take a view on it on the basis of certain general ideas or of expertise in other disciplines (New Testament, Church history, etc.). And so we have the dicta that Heidegger "introduces temporality into the idea of God" (!) or that "he ontologizes death" (!), dicta that exclude the possibility of serious dialogue. What Greek "intellectuals" have written on the "ontology of the person" is quite literally crazy in its simplistic and arbitrary nature.

I believe, if I am not mistaken, that reservations expressed in the West derive on the one hand from ignorance of my work *Person and Eros* (which was issued in English only in 2007—thirty-seven years after its first edition in Greek—and which has never been published in French), and on the other from the assumption created by rumor of my project. An Orthodox engaging with Heidegger? Why else, but clearly to draw from Heidegger's critique of Western metaphysical weapons to use against the West! They do not consider that a Greek of today lives, thinks, and searches for meaning using the terms of the Western "paradigm," and that he fell in love with Heidegger because in his own struggle he found an Ariadne's thread leading him to the rediscovery of the Greek otherness that has been preserved in ecclesial Orthodoxy. I have lived, my dear Norman, in Paris for five years. I taught for two years at St Sergius. The francophone Orthodox community of Paris became for me a second home. But my friends there always held me in a kind of quarantine, always kept me under observation. I was for them the "anti-Westerner." The very few translations of my more popular books received notice, and these alone. My work has remained unknown in France.

Apophaticism as an Epistemological Principle

NR: *You have defined apophaticism as the refusal to exhaust knowledge by its formulation, the refusal to identify the understanding of the signifiers with the knowledge of the things signified. You see this as the key to avoiding relativism and agnosticism, the key to the experiential verification of knowledge. Is apophaticism, then, simply a recognition that reality extends beyond that which is constructed by language? If that is the case, how does apophaticism differ from agnosticism?*

CY: Agnosticism is a thesis (*thēsis*); apophaticism is an attitude (*stasis*). The thesis expresses a watertight certainty that functions as an ideological, atomic conviction: "I am persuaded that I cannot know whether any metaphysical reality actually exists; I have neither the power nor the means of attaining such knowledge." Thus the subject of metaphysical reality or of its nonexistence ceases to present itself as a problem. There is no margin for posing questions or making an investigation. The adoption of such an impervious and closed certainty is what we call *agnosticism*.

Apophaticism is an *attitude*: "I am open to the possibility that that which I wish to know may exist or not exist. But I identify this possible knowledge (from experience) with *empirical verification*, not with the *understanding* of the linguistic signifiers of what is sought." Apophaticism does not simply refer to the linguistic signifiers of metaphysics; it is a general epistemological *principle*. It insists on the difference between the signifiers and what they signify, on the difference between the form of knowledge conveyed by the understanding of the signifiers and the experiential knowledge of the things signified.

I like to give the following example: A child that has lost its mother at the time of its birth understands the intellectual content of the term "maternal love" but does not *know* maternal love. Someone may have learned the rules of swimming by heart but may have never plunged into the sea. Such a person does not *know* what swimming is.

The *attitude* of apophaticism, as I have shown in my books, is an epistemological principle that since antiquity has characterized the Greek tradition. This attitude presupposed the *social verification* of knowledge, the Heraclitean dictum "that which we share we verify; that which we possess privately we falsify"—knowledge is verified "when all share the same opinion and each witnesses to it experientially" (Aristotle). The etymological sense of the Greek word for "truth," *a-lēthia*, is characteristic. The word is put together from the privative alpha and *lēthē* ("concealment"). *A-lēthia* is non-*lēthē*, nonconcealment. Consequently, "appearance" (*emphaneia*) or "manifestation" (*phanerōsis*) is a "coming to light." By the faculty of sight, we have our most direct experience of participation in reality. It is not at all by chance that the ancient Greek words concerning the way knowledge works refer to the sense of *sight*: we speak of *ideas*, and of form or *eidos* (from *idein*, "to see"), of *theory* (from *theōrein*, "to behold"), of *phenomena* (from *phainein*, "to bring to light")—and even the verb *phēmi* ("I say") comes from *piphauskō* ("I make manifest").

The twin expressions "apophaticism" and "social verification of knowledge" differentiate Greek epistemology from the epistemology that shaped the post-Roman (barbarian) West. And because the difference between *modes of life*, that is, between *cultures*, is shaped by the prevailing epistemology in any society (not by its ontology), the whole civilization of the post-Roman West was shaped along lines quite different from the Greek *mode*.

A characteristic example is this: whereas for a Greek, *truth* is an experience of vision, a participation in appearance/manifestation, for a Westerner, truth is the "coincidence of the thing thought with the concept" (*adaequatio rei et intellectus*). The coincidence of the object with its intellectual conception in my understanding defines and exhausts the truth. The intellect alone suffices for the knowledge and appropriation of truth; the intellectual conception is the real existent, not its sensory verification (hence the Cartesian axiom: *cogito ergo sum*).

NR: *You make the point very forcefully that epistemologically what we share in, we verify, whereas what we grasp as individuals is subject to illusion. But why should it be axiomatic that the social is more reliable than the individual? Did not ideologies such as fascism and communism claim social verification?*

CY: First, the totalitarian regimes did not claim the *verification* of their ideology, but its *reception* by all—and the religionized Christian confessions demand the same thing. The principle of the social or communitarian verification of knowledge wants atomic empirical testimonies to coincide (i.e., the experience itself to be shared), so that then we should receive the coincidence/sharing as confirmation of the truth. It is one thing if affirmation arises from the personal experience of each of us and is verified only when it coincides with the empirical affirmation of everybody else; it is something radically different if truth is put forward as a given (as in ideology) and its acceptance is required of everybody. In the first case we have a supreme event of freedom, in the second a typical symptom of illiberal authoritarian imposition.

Communitarian verification is something other than collective or mass acceptance. The former is an achievement of breaking free from the egocentric instinctive need of the possession of "truth," an achievement of *relation* (of reception/communion) with the empirical affirmation of our fellow human beings too. The latter is an abandonment of freedom, a shoring up of the egocentric demand to possess the "truth" with "objective" guarantees (of authority, systematic proof, manifest utility, etc.).

Common experience confirms that atomic empirical affirmation easily slides into illusion—it is easily influenced by what is desired psychologically, by what satisfies the appetite for pleasure, and so forth. The communitarian verification of atomic affirmations, however, is not an easy recipe: like every event of relations of communion, it is the product of a struggle for freedom from the instinctive tendency toward egotistic self-affirmation and self-sufficiency, an achievement of breaking free from existential individualism, with the aim of receiving and coordinating ourselves empirically with the testimony of the experiential witness of the others. The struggle for verification is existential; the field of verification is language.

NR: *When you first published your* Postmodern Metaphysics *twenty years ago, you believed that developments in quantum physics had opened up new possibilities for metaphysical thinking. Have you seen any encouraging signs that this has been the case?*

CY: I continue to believe that new possibilities have indeed been opened up. But it is not at all evident that these possibilities have been exploited. The philosophical appropriation of the "relationalist" approach to reality post-Newtonian physics introduced (and of the analogous language that it employed) must perhaps come from academic circles acceptable in the West. If the attempt to exploit such possibilities originates in the "margins" (outside the established centers) of Western thinking, it will encounter indifference and prejudice. I remember Zissimos Lorentzatos once speaking to me about the "provincialism" of the West. I was astonished at the time, but my experience since then has proved him right. You too, my dear Norman, will remember how many British and American publishers rejected your English translation of *Postmodern Metaphysics*. They were simply not interested. I have two heavy files of rejections from the publishers we approached. I have come to see that books of topical interest in a journalistic style are acceptable in the West, whoever may have written them, if they concern symptomatic aspects of the dead ends of the Western "paradigms." But books offering a critique of the philosophical presuppositions of this "paradigm" find access to the Western publishing market closed to them.

I venture to believe that my book *Person and Eros* is the first and only consistent counterproposition to Heidegger's ontology—a systematic synthesis, in modern epistemological terms, of the ontological hermeneutic proposition of the Hellenic-ecclesial "mode." It was published in your English translation in April 2008 (seven years ago). In these seven years, I do not know of a single review that has been able to attract broader academic interest. Perhaps it takes time for a book to bear fruit. Or maybe all that is needed is a series of coincidences.

NR: *The philosophy of religion as taught in universities in Britain and the United States is mainly to do with arguments for and against the existence of God. How do you approach the philosophy of religion in a way that does not treat God simply as an object of mind, and yet make it acceptable in the academy?*

CY: To what extent the term "philosophy of religion" is tied to the demands of formal logic, or what semantic content it actually aspires to, is a topic I won't discuss here. Let us dwell, rather, on your very important observation that the anthropological form of the Western "paradigm" has for centuries constantly revolved around arguments *for* or *against* the existence of God.

Yes, because it seeks the verification of knowledge, of information, of the intellectual *suppositio*—either in syllogistic demonstration, or in the authority of a transcendent principle, or in the authority of a method. For centuries now, Western thinkers have ignored verification through communal experience, through relationship-participation in the sharing of common experience.

I recall a well-known female journalist who interviewed me one evening on Greek television. We were discussing the social crisis in Greece today and its cultural and anthropological consequences. Suddenly, and without any real connection with the logical flow of our discussion, the journalist asked me playfully, in a rather pointed manner, "Do you really believe in God?"

Reacting spontaneously, I said at once, "Do *you* believe in Mozart?" And I explained: I know Mozart because I know and love his work. In his work I discover the otherness of the *personal* existence of Mozart—the unique, dissimilar, and unrepeatable character of his person. I know him with much greater immediacy and reality than did, say, some contemporary neighbor of his who met him every day in the street but did not know his musical compositions.

Faith (trust) in God is an experience of *relation*, not an intellectual certainty. Relation begins with the discovery of his personal otherness in the beauty and wisdom of sensible reality—in the same way that we discover a painter through his painting and a composer through his music. And this knowledge that is conveyed by the relation has the constantly perfected, and never fully realized, dynamic of erotic love. The question "Do you believe in God?" means (at least in the Greek language): "Do you trust him?" And to trust him, you must know him, at least from his work, in the degree required to win your confidence. From that point, the knowledge of his person is as unbounded as knowledge is in the case of a human person: it is constantly perfected without ever reaching its limit.

Arguments *for* and *against* the existence of God refer to individual "convictions," ideological viewpoints, and psychological choices, not to the *knowledge* of God. They keep us tied to an infantile level—I would venture to say that the "philosophy of religion," if it poses such a problem of arguments *for* and *against*, is pure childishness.

Essence and Energies

NR: *Central to your approach is the distinction between the essence and the energies of God. Yet this is an idea that, despite able advocacy by people such as David Bradshaw, meets with great resistance in the West. Do you see this resistance as one of the barriers to serious philosophical discussion of the arguments you present?*

CY: You see, my dear Norman, how even you, a serious student of the ecclesial tradition, can speak of the "support" of an "approach" by sharp intellects such as that of David Bradshaw. We are all children of the West, embodying its mental outlook. But the distinction between *essence* and the *energies* of the essence is not simply a methodological tool, a *mode* of relation with reality. If we attempt to know existents with regard to their essence, we have no other means of doing so apart from our individual intellects, in which case we end up in the a priori speculativeness of dogmas and authority. But if the *essence* is a *mode* by which what is, *is active* existentially, then the knowledge of the mode is possible only as *participation*, as experience of relation.

That is why distinguishing between *essence* and *energies* or rejecting the distinction is a difference not of "approaches," or methods, or "spiritualities," but of cultures, of *modes* of life. The *mode* shaped by the post-Roman West is incompatible with the *mode* of the Church—just as the *mode* of individualism, of self-interest, is incompatible with the *mode* of love. This way of putting it may seem provocative, but we should not forget that I am putting it so as a child of the West. It is a form of self-criticism—painful, but perhaps liberating too.

NR: *Aristotle Papanikolaou raises an interesting question that is indirectly but clearly addressed to you. He says, "The basic question is: if divine–human communion is conceptualized in terms of the essence/energies distinction, then what's the point of the* Logos? *Why affirm God as Trinity? I simply cannot accept Lossky's answer that it is a* primordial *fact. I agree more with Rahner (and Zizioulas) in stating that God's being as Trinity* is *God's freedom to be in communion with what is not God, and this communion is in the* Logos *by the Holy Spirit. God's freedom to be in communion with what is not God is the* Logos, *who is distinct from the Father and the Holy Spirit, and is* not *the energies that are distinct from the essence. Divine–human communion is in the end a* hypostatic *event, not an* energetic one."[5] *How would you respond to this?*

CY: Permit me, my dear Norman, first of all to replace the verb "to conceptualize" in Papanikolaou's statement with the verb "to signify." What we are seeking to do is not to "conceptualize" the reality (the fact) of a *relation* (divine-human communion), but to be able to signify it (simply in an indicative manner) in the terms of our language, whose limits are clearly the limits of created reality (the limits of our world, as Wittgenstein says).

The *relation* (or communion) between Creator and created being cannot be signified linguistically by the terms "essence" and "energies" of the essence, for these terms are not determinative of *relation*; they are determinative of *existence*. By these two

[5]Aristotle Papanikolaou in a personal communication to Norman Russell. Cf. *Being with God: Trinity, Apophaticism, and Divine-Human Communion* (Notre Dame, IN: University of Notre Dame Press, 2006), 121–27.

terms ("essence" and "energies") we signify, in our relative and inadequate language, the *mode* of *being* of the two terms of the divine-human relation, not the fact itself of their relation. What is "antecedent" (in the logic of our language) is that which divinity *is* and that which humanity *is*; then comes the signifying of the fact of their *relation*.

Of course, the *relation* between God and humanity is possible (always subject to the relative powers of human reason) because the essence-nature of both, the *mode* of their existence (in the way we know this experientially as an *active* mode), is *rational*, that is to say, it is ek-static, manifested, offered to us to be known and participated in. By the words "essence" and "energies," we indicate the fundamental presupposition and capacity of their mode of existence, whereas by the word "relation" (or "communion"), we indicate the consequence, the resultant fact of the *mode*.

The one God is *Logos* (an existent, hypostatic reality that is revealed, offered to be known and participated in). The same one God is also *Father* (an existent hypostatic reality that is absolute cause, freedom from any causal predetermination of existence). The same one God is also *Holy Spirit* (an existent hypostatic reality whose identity is that of active and given self-offering). It is difficult, almost impossible, for us, within the limits of our creaturely reasoning and experience, to conceive of the *hypostasis* of what exists (the specific and active realization of existence) as free from the terms and limitations of atomicity, to conceive of it as operative as the freedom of loving otherness without any presuppositions. That is also why certain linguistic expressions of the incarnate *Logos* seem strange to us, expressions such as "I and the Father are one" (Jn 10.30), "He who has seen me has seen the Father" (Jn 14.9), and "The Father is in me and I in him" (Jn 10.38), and so on.

"Why affirm God as Trinity?" asks Papanikolaou. And he replies, "God's being as Trinity *is* God's freedom to be in communion with what is not God, and this communion is *in* the *Logos by* the Holy Spirit." But if God's *mode* of existence (triadicity) is determined by the necessity for God to be in communion with what is not God, then what is not God is ontologically prior to God: it determines God's *being* as a necessity.

I would hold that to say that God's communion with what is not God (the fact of the *relation* of the Creator with creatures) is realized "*in* the *Logos by* the Holy Spirit" does not adequately express ecclesial experience. What does "in" the *Logos* and "by" the Holy Spirit mean? Does the *Logos* hypostasize the necessity of God's communion with what is not God? And does this hypostasization of God's relation with the world have its cause (its originating principle) in the Spirit, rather than in the Father?

The Church's theology is summed up in John's definition: "God is love" (1 Jn 4.16). Love is not an idiom, or property, of God, a moral quality belonging to him, or a behavioral category. It is the *mode* by which he exists. He exists because he freely wills to exist, and he wills to exist because he loves. His free will is the "act," the "fact," the "mode" of his existence: he "begets" the Son-*Logos* and causes the Spirit to "proceed." God hypostasizes his being as freedom of love; the names "Father," "Son," and "Spirit" refer to the hypostasization (realization) of existence as loving *relation* (the fullness of freedom)—not as individual entities bounded by the necessary reason (determinative) of their existence (like the names Zeus, Kronos, Uranus, etc.).

Ecclesial triadology (ontology) is nullified if we limit God's freedom simply to his power of relating to, or being in communion with, what is not God—if we limit this power to a *hypostatic* fact, with the person of the Son-Logos hypostasizing this divine power in an exclusive manner. Ecclesial triadology is nullified if it is not the common *energies* of the monarchical Trinity that realize not only the unified summons of divine love that gives beings hypostasis out of nonbeing, but also humanity's participation in the *mode* of the uncreated.

I can understand the statement that God's relationship with beings (the active summoning of beings from nonbeing into being) hypostasizes existents, that it endows them with a created hypostasis ("The divine will became the matter and substance of created things" [Gregory of Nyssa, PG 44:1312A]).[6] The common activity (energy) of the freedom of the three persons of the Trinity—their active will—"is immediately substantiated, having become the nature" (Basil the Great, PG 29:736C). And I can understand the statement that the positive response of human freedom (the "yes," the "amen") to the summons to what is "in the likeness" is capable of being made hypostatic because this capacity has been inaugurated by the Son's voluntary inhomination "by the good pleasure of the Father" and "the cooperation of the Holy Spirit." Divine-human communion or relation is realized hypostatically in the person of Christ and operates hypostatically through the common will-energy of the Trinity, just as it also operates in the person of every human being who strives to coordinate his or her freedom with the freedom of the Son and *Logos*.

Any attempt to promote the Thomist rejection of the distinction between *essence* and the essence's *energies*, to replace the empirical realism of this distinction with an intellectualist Aristotelian version of God's essence as "pure act," nullifies the pragmatic character of ecclesial experience and witness.

The case of the human being (the image of God) adequately clarifies the ontological difference that is reflected in the distinction between *essence* and the essence's *energies*: every human being possesses thought, judgment, imagination, will, and desire, as well as the capacity for bipedal motion, laughter, and so on. All

---

[6]J. P. Migne, Patrologiae Cursus Completus, Series Graeca (Paris: Migne, 1857–66); cited as PG.

these marks are characteristics of every human being; they deter-mine the common *mode* of existence of humankind, and they define humankind's *essence*. But they would have been abstract definitions if they did not operate in a practical way in every human being, that is, if their empirical attestation did not point to the energies-powers of every human being, to the marks of the *essence* of humankind. All human beings possess thought, judgment, imagination, will, and so forth. These active ("ener-getic") powers-capacities characterize the essence-nature (mode) of humankind. Every human being, however, acts (thinks, judges, imagines, wills, etc.) in a unique, dissimilar, and unrepeatable way—the existential reality both of the *essence* and of the *ener-gies* of the essence is always hypostatic.

The Neopatristic Project

NR: *I wonder if one reason why your work is not widely reviewed in the West, Christos, apart from a perceived "anti-Westernism," isn't the way in which patristic studies are conducted in the West. In England the revival of interest in the Fathers in the nineteenth century had an apologetic purpose, to minimize the significance of the Anglican Church's sixteenth-century breach with Rome by demonstrating a continuity of faith with the Church of the early centuries. In recent decades, however, patristic studies have become a scholarly discipline of their own, more or less detached from current theological concerns, indeed almost a branch of Late Antique studies. In a not entirely dissimilar way, in the Roman Catholic Church the postwar recovery of the Greek Fathers was a means of attacking the dominant neo-Thomism by appealing to sources that could not be officially censured. I have the impres-sion that in this case too, the Fathers are treated largely as histori-cal testimonies to an earlier stage of the evolution of Christianity. The Fathers have a different role in Orthodoxy, haven't they?*

CY: Your observation, I think, is an interesting one. Certainly, if we look back critically at the phenomenon that we have called "returning to the Fathers," "neopatristic theology," or whatever else, we can identify ulterior motives, whether conscious or unconscious. But I cannot believe that these were the motives that gave rise to phenomenon. They may have played a role in its retrospective exploitation, but the interest that led to the "discovery" of the Fathers cannot have been anything but genuine and firsthand.

The contribution of the émigré Russians was, I believe, vital, especially that of Fr George Florovsky, Vladimir Lossky, and Fr John Meyendorff. I would go so far as to say that Lossky's *Mystical Theology of the Eastern Church* is the most important work of ecclesiastical literature since the fourteenth century and St Gregory Palamas.[7] It came quite out of the blue. I am at a loss to say which persons or what book prepared the way. The most probably explanation is that the Russian diaspora needed to demonstrate to the West (where it found itself transplanted involuntarily) the identity-difference of the Orthodox ecclesial tradition. And it sought this identity-difference in the Fathers of the Church up to the fourteenth century—where else, since what had prevailed from that time in both Russia and the Greek world was the "Babylonian captivity," or dependency on the Western outlook: thralldom to individualism-rationalism, that is to say, to the *religionization* of the ecclesial event.

But in the West too, the "discovery" of the Eastern Fathers must, in a first phase that differs from one country to another, have started from a sincere need for the witness of the Church to reconnect with existential experience, for theology to reject its academic-formalistic and moralistic-utilitarian character. Of course the recovery of the Fathers did not arrive at the point of

---

[7]Vladimir Lossky, *The Mystical Theology of the Eastern Church* (Crestwood, NY: St Vladimir's Seminary Press, 1991). The original French version was published in 1944; the English translation was first issued in 1957.

casting doubt on the main features of the "religionization" of the ecclesial event in the West, that is, the wholesale dominance of Augustine and Aquinas in the historical development of Western Christianity. It opened up new horizons, however, in historical theology and constituted a historical event that marked the twentieth century.

My personal experience, although it does not lay claim to any objective validity, testifies to how precious the (direct and indirect) patristic approach and theological perspective of Western theologians has been for my generation. I am thinking of Anglicans such as Archbishop Michael Ramsey, Fr Derwas Chitty, Donald Allchin, and George Every, and of how stimulating and fruitful we found the studies of Roman Catholics such as Daniélou, Henri de Lubac, Louis Bouyer, von Balthasar, and de Gandillac.

Certainly, this "discovery" of patristic wisdom and experience did not endure, but declined suddenly and dramatically. After the first generation of émigré Russians driven westward by the Bolsheviks, a generation that strove to manifest and witness to the otherness of Orthodoxy, the second and third generations, in contrast, were afraid of insisting on otherness. Now born, raised, and educated within Western communities, they felt there was a primary necessity to prove that the ecclesial (Orthodox) *mode* of existence was not incompatible with the individualistic-utilitarian *mode* of existence of Western civilization—Orthodoxy is simply a more "spiritual," more "mystical" tendency within a "unified" Christianity, preserving more ancient traditions of individual piety, a richer and more evocative form of liturgy, and more "impressionistic" expressions of art. They held that it is wrong for us to believe that Western civilization was shaped principally by the Augustinism of Charlemagne (i.e., of Alcuin) and of Pope Gregory I, or by Descartes, Propaganda Fidei, and Index Librorum Prohibitorum, because the civilization of the West was also shaped by Cluny, the Cistercians, and Pascal.

The "school" of "neopatristic" Roman Catholic theologians was systematically neutralized by the Vatican, especially after the Second Vatican Council, which was regarded as excessively influenced by pro-Orthodox novelties. An organized effort to preserve Vatican II's "climate" of fruitful openness to the Tradition of the undivided Church found expression in the journal *Concilium*. It was published in seven languages and was directed by internationally renowned figures in Roman Catholic theology: Schillebeeckx, Congar, Chenu, Rahner, Duquoc, Hans Küng, Metz, and David Tracy. Gradually and imperceptibly the journal developed into a platform for the radically Protestantized theses of a "theology" concerned exclusively with giving a "religious" view on topics set by contemporary secular interests (the demands of the feminist movement and of Latin American revolutionary groups, the problems of democracy and of the social exercise of power, etc.).

I think that the *Concilium* experiment showed clearly that whatever the "openness" of the West to the undivided Church's past, if it takes place à la carte (picking out bits that appeal to you), it is doomed to be confined to the trajectory always followed by every evasion, invalidation, or alienation of the ecclesial event for the sake of religious, moral, or simply utilitarian motives. For about ten years, I experienced the tragic course taken by *Concilium* as a member of its editorial board (*comité de direction*). I recall my desperate attempts to bring into the planning of the issues, even in a rudimentary form, some discussion of the existential "meaning," of the ontological reality, of the hope that "death should be trampled on by death." They used to listen to me with sincere interest, satisfied that the "pluralism" of the company also included "the Orthodox point of view," but they returned to the topics that concerned them, the ideological elaboration of contemporary problems unrelated to the illumination of "meaning."

I am inclined to believe that the development of "neopatristic theology" in Greece was not very different. The beginnings, at least as I experienced them personally through contact with Dimitrios Koutroubis, had the joy—not to say the intoxication—of the discovery of a testimony to the Church's experience that liberated one from the chattering vacuities of the religious ideologizing that was tormenting humanity. This was a testimony that was freed from legalism.

It was not long, however, before the "return to the Fathers" was assimilated to the terms of a theologizing imposed by what was in practice the Westernization of Greek society. The "return to the Fathers" was subordinated to the priorities of Greece's secondhand academicism and pietism. The pietistic movements, which monopolized religious life in the last century without anybody protesting, saw in the patristic texts the possibility of broadening their recourse to an "inspired" authority that shored up the individual with certainties. It was no longer Scripture alone, but now the Fathers too (a patristic phrase, a brief gobbet), that sufficed as incontrovertible "proof" of "orthodoxy." A neoscholasticism, now on the basis of the Fathers rather than of Aristotle or Scripture, became the central characteristic and methodological choice of academic theology. It was sufficient (and still is) for anyone to catalog the texts of a church father (or simply a single text), linking his references to a specific concept or term and arranging his entries according to a rudimentary synthetic unity, for this person to be awarded the title of doctor of theology and, almost invariably, to be appointed to an academic post.

The "recovery of the Fathers" is, I believe, one of the basic reasons for the depreciation and discrediting of the schools of theology in Greek universities during the last thirty years.

NR: *You have often been associated with Florovsky, Lossky, and the neopatristic school of theology, who sought to find new ways of expressing what the Church has always taught. Yet to me you also*

*seem to share something of the approach of the Russian school
(Bulgakov, Zenkovsky, and others) who attempted to reconstruct
Orthodoxy in engagement with modern ideas. How do you view
the impact of these two schools on the development of Orthodox
theology in the twentieth century? Would the phrase "thinking
with the fathers beyond the fathers" (used by Papanikolaou with
reference to Zizioulas) also characterize your own work?*

CY: Let me first express my opposition to schematizations that
assume that theology is not testimony to ecclesial experience, but
to ideology. Only ideologies seek to "reconstruct Orthodoxy in
engagement with modern ideas" or to "find new ways of expressing" themselves. Have you ever heard of any "school" or group of
intellectuals formed to "reconstruct" love, or to find "new ways"
of expressing it? The history of humanity knows nothing of this;
it only recognizes those people of experience who witness to the
wonder of love and celebrate it, and those loveless people who
"study" love as a sociological, psychological, and moral subject.

If Florovsky, Lossky, Meyendorff, Schmemann, and Zizioulas
have anything in common, it is because they have become aware
(each by his own route) that the texts of the Fathers of the Church
are not just another source of "infallible" ideological principles,
but a settling down of personal testimony to their grappling with
ecclesial experience. Bulgakov, Zenkovsky, and Berdyaev were
more enclosed within a theory of the Church's gospel, a theory
of a historical, ideological, and effectual character.

I suspect that by "thinking with the fathers *beyond* the fathers,"
Aristotle Papanikolaou wants to draw attention to the danger
of attributing a "divine inspiration" to the Fathers, such as that
which the Protestants attribute to Scripture, so that we regard
them as an "infallible" source of ideological Orthodoxy—rather
like the way Marxists approach the writings of Karl Marx, or
Freudians, the writings of Sigmund Freud. If one had any inkling,
even a rudimentary one, of what the ecclesial event is and what

the witness of *its* experience is, then one would reject all these expressions—"neopatristic theology," "return to the Fathers," "postpatristic theology," and so on—as equally trite products of the ideological alienation of the "pearl of great price."

Contextual Theology

NR: *I think you are right that Papanikolaou's intention is to oppose a fundamentalist approach to the Fathers. In reaction to such fundamentalism, there are Orthodox theologians who now talk about "contextual theology." This has not always been well received in Greece. Metropolitan Paul of Glyfada, for example, has recently issued an open letter criticizing a theological approach that seems to him to relativize the Fathers, making them nonnormative for Orthodoxy. Do you share his concerns?*

CY: I am not familiar with the content of Metropolitan Paul of Glyfada's open letter. I know that this metropolitan does not have much to do with ecclesial theology. He is a typical functionary satisfying people's religious needs, with a rather strange psychology and a tendency toward zealotry. I am familiar, however, with an excellent, in my opinion, ecclesial theological text which was published in the journal *Synaxi* (116 [October–December 2010]: 101–6). It is by Presbyter George Anagnostopoulos, a professor in the Electrical and Computer Engineering Department of the Democritus University of Thrace, and expresses both his affirmations of the term "neopatristic synthesis" and his abomination of the term "postpatristic theology."

Those who profess to consider the Fathers today in a *contextual* context have taken a shine to the fashion for investigating a contextual hermeneutic, prevalent in the nihilistic tendencies of self-proclaimed "postmodernity" and impervious to any other kind of investigation apart from the attempt to relativize not what is by definition a relative-symbolic linguistic expression, but the fact itself of shared experience, of socially validated (through communal relations) experiential knowledge.

The devotees in Greece of contextual hermeneutics (which they translate, in inept Greek, as "*synapheiakē theologia*"!) are thus led to proclaim that theology needs to be liberated from the cultural framework of patristic and conciliar Tradition that is Greek philosophy and a communitarian perspective. Of course they deride the attempt to reply in the language of ecclesial experience to the questions posed by the nihilistic ontology of Heidegger, or they also deride the debates that were conducted in the 1960s in the journal *Synoro* in issues dedicated to such subjects as Orthodoxy and politics, Orthodox and modern art, Orthodoxy and Marxism, Orthodoxy and nationalism, and so on.

It is abundantly clear that "contextual" theology is not interested in how we can witness today to "Christ and the power of his resurrection" (Phil 3.10), the existential meaning of the experience that death "has been trampled on by death"—nothing of this. "Contextual" theology is interested in modish attention seeking: in theology's instituting a dialogue with our multicultural society and accepting the terms of the "pluralism" of views and institutionalized "tolerance" of every distortion, falsification, and perversion of the hope of the gospel.

I need not go on. In no age and in no cultural "paradigm" have people who are serious in their inquiries, whether metaphysical or textual, bothered with such a pathetic hunt for publicity. Besides, as I have said, Fr George Anagnostopoulos's text deals with the matter very fully.

NR: *May I press you a little further, Christos, on your own hermeneutic principles? Many of your books reveal an engagement with the Fathers that is very creative. You do not simply cite their words as authorities supporting some theological position that has been reached on rationalist grounds (the scholastic method you have so often criticized). You explore the witness of the Fathers in relation* to our participation in the fact of the Church, our experience of the ecclesial body. This, of course, has not always been well received by academic theologians. For example, the thesis you presented many years ago to the University of Athens on The Metaphysics of the Body, subtitled A Study of John Climacus, shocked the professors of that time, if I am not mistaken, on account of an approach to the experience of the Church that was entirely unfamiliar to them and clashed with their scholastic principles. More recently, in your books Relational Ontology and The Enigma of Evil, you argue that in the light of what has been established by modern science, the fall can no longer be considered a historical event. This, of course, is not controversial for anyone except fundamentalists. But you go further and say that the fall cannot even be considered a symbolic event in the traditional sense of humanity's willful alienation from God. It can only stand for humanity's very createdness. What the Church offers is therefore not simply reconciliation with God on the moral level, or some kind of justification in legal terms, but freedom from createdness itself. I find this a very exciting vision of the Church's mission that builds on Maximus the Confessor's balancing of creation and theōsis. But is this not "contextual" theology in the acceptable sense of interpreting the Fathers in the light of our own experience?

CY: It is useful, in my view, Norman, that in our discussion we should keep to firm definitions of the semantic content of words in order to avoid confusion. Let us accept then as our definition of "contextual" theology only that which is given by its principal advocates in Greece, namely, that "contextual" theology is the theology that "takes place in a specific historical and cultural context as a response to specific questions and challenges posed by the historical conditions and the sociopolitical debates of any given period, so that theology is in dialogue with the broader social and cultural realities of the age" (*Synaxi* 113 [January–February 2010]: 35–36).

I appreciate the need that gives rise to this definition: that we should not regard "an abstract theology with a catholic and global validity, that is, some kind of nonhistorical, immutable, timeless, and monolithic tradition, as serving the truth of the gospel." But is the alternative to such a formulation the "topicalization" of theology, "the reply to specific questions" in a different way in every age and in every culture?

Unless I am mistaken, that which we call the Church's theology is a witness to its experience. It begins with the witness of the apostles to the historical person of Christ. His disciples and the apostles witness that in the case of this person, "the boundaries of nature have been overcome": the laws/necessities governing created animate life have been abrogated/annihilated. Christ is not a natural individual endowed with supernatural powers (a "fakir" who performs "miracles"), but an existence free from any determination of nature or essence. He is a human being free (and able to render his fellow humans free) from subjection to nature's heaviness, nature's decay, and nature's finitude (e.g., in the case of the five loaves and two fishes), and he is finally free from death. This existential freedom of his is confirmed by specific "signs," by practical manifestations of freedom.

Christ says of himself that he is the *Son Logos* (manifestation) of *God the Father*; that he was "sent" to manifest God to humanity as *Father*, *Son*, and consoling *Spirit*. These three words, "Father," "Son," and "Spirit," make their appearance in the Christian "*kērygma*" from the very beginning. They (and these three alone) constitute the "good news" of the Church, the announcement of joy that those who had experienced the historical presence of Christ bring to the world.

What "joy" do these three words bring? The proclamation, subjected to experiential confirmation, that the Causal Principle of existence and of that which exists is not an inexplicable given "divinity," an entity predetermined by axiomatic necessity to be that which it is (Being in an ultimate sense, divine, most exalted genus, transcendent power, etc.)—it is not the Causal Principle of that which exists in the sense of a blind necessity. It is a self-conscious, rational (communicating) existence, free from any predetermination, self-determined existentially as freedom of love. It exists because it wills to exists, and it realizes its free will in *hypostases* that exist because they love and only in order to love. That is why they can be signified in human language not by the signifiers of individual entities (Zeus, Apollo, or Hephaestus), but by names that reveal *relation:* fatherhood, sonship, unity, and difference.

The historical Jesus, the anointed of God, confirms by his existence that God is free from his divinity, and for that reason can also without change or alteration exist as a human being, free also from the limitations of humanity, as his resurrection from the dead testifies. His freedom from existential limitations is not a necessary property; it is a fact of free will, the *mode* of love, a mode of divine existential freedom "grafted" (Rom 11.17) into human nature, given as a potentiality to humanity's existence.

Church—*ecclesia*—is the realization of this divine gift constituted by the incarnation of God: it is the mode of the Trinity, the mode of freedom from every existential necessity, made a reality from created human existences—it is existence as relation; existence as love, resurrection, and immortality; existence as a gift of God freely and actively received by humanity. Both in the triadic God and in the ecclesial human being, will or freedom is not an individual property, something exercised or achieved, but a fact and realization of relation self-transcendence—it is love as *mode of existence.*

Consequently, the Church's gospel, the witness of ecclesial experience, does not have elements dependent on their historical "context" in a specific culture, so that when the culture changes, it is inevitably required that the significance of ecclesial experience should also change. The Church through the centuries does not bear ideas, propositions, or hermeneutical views on God and metaphysics. The Church only sets down its experience that if the mode of existence changes—if humanity wishes to exist and struggles to do so only in order to love and because it loves, if it fights to free itself from the ego—then its life becomes a celebration, a foretaste of the freedom that Christ granted to human nature.

The only changeable element in this deposit of ecclesial witness is language. Only the language of *relation*, the expression of love, can constantly be altered and renewed without the power of new expression ever being exhausted. Humanity continues to produce erotic literature, love poetry, because human beings continue to exist who actively live love and witness to it—no one has thought of demanding that love poetry should have a "historical context" with topical historico-social (mutable) conditions.

There are two distinct groups that hold absolutely the same puerile sense of the "gospel" as ideology: (1) so-called conservatives who make an idol of the letter of the patristic formulations because they need to clad their ego in "certainties" (the "zealots," "ultra-Orthodox," "integrists," and "defenders of dogma and the canons"); and (2) the so-called "progressives" or "modernists," who engage in "dialogues" with, or "openings" toward, every "culture" and every "new trend." The members of both these groups are victims of the same individualistic religionization of the ecclesial fact. If you wish, we can discuss this. The different readings of John Climacus you refer to are a very characteristic example.

The Mode of the Created and the Mode of the Uncreated

NR: *In this connection, could I bring you back to* The Metaphysics of the Body *and to your proposition concerning the nature of evil in* The Enigma of Evil? *You express radical views in these books that call for further elucidation.*

CY: You are right, I left what you had asked me about the *Metaphysics of the Body* and the *Enigma of Evil* unanswered. I am grateful for the question, because no one before has asked for clarification on these matters.

When in January 1966 I submitted the *Metaphysics of the Body* as a doctoral dissertation to the Theological Faculty of the University of Athens, the kind of thesis that sought to present the views of a particular church father on a particular topic had only just begun to appear. It was, I would say, the period in which we were discovering the new things that the witness of the ecclesial experience of the Fathers was conveying to us—new in comparison with the intellectualist stereotypes that an academicism imitative of the West had imposed upon theology. We were still in the period of surprise: we were discovering with enthusiasm in the texts of the Fathers a language and an approach to problems that lent a completely different character to theological research from that to which we had become accustomed in our university studies.

This research had not yet been "categorized," had not yet been "formatted" in terms of what would later be called "neopatristic theology." That is to say, the study of the Fathers had not yet been gnawed at by the established outlook of regarding as "scientific" that which can be shored up with references and transformed into an "infallible" authority: in the divinely inspired Scriptures or in the Fathers of a similarly axiomatic validity. (Today the most Protestantized party in "Orthodoxy" is made up of the so-called "zealots," or "genuine Orthodox," or "extreme conservatives," who have turned the Fathers into idols in the way that Protestants have idolized Scripture, with a view to armorplating their ego with certainty, validity, and the arrogance of being in possession of the invincible truth that "conquers all.")

I chose *The Ladder* of John of Sinai because by general consent it was regarded as one of the most "austere" ascetical texts, one of the least compatible with any affirmation of materiality, of the body and the natural desires. In the course of studying the text, I became increasingly convinced that yes, there were many reasons why one should infer a Platonizing and even Manichean hostility to matter and the body, but at the same time one could discern an entirely nonfortuitous insistence on principles that radically refuted a Platonic or Manichean dualism—for example, (1) that a human being is a totality of soul and spirit; that Christ enthroned human flesh in the glory of the Godhead; (2) that the material nature of humanity is not by origin "evil": the passions are a distortion of good natural impulses, the natural impulses becomes passions because they are subordinated to the priority of the ego; (3) that erotic desire and power is the natural presupposition of love for one's neighbor and ultimately for God; (4) that the final destiny of our material body is that it should acquire "glory"—the manifestation of the *mode* of divine existence and life; (5) that the body should participate in this *mode*; and (6) that the material flesh of humanity should be *deified*.

I have the impression, perhaps mistakenly, that this was the first time that the then professors of the Theological Faculty of the University of Athens had encountered a theological hermeneutics and language of this kind, and one indeed drawn from a patristic text of the ascetical corpus. It was therefore natural that they should react as if it were a misunderstanding and misinterpretation of the text. They referred the thesis back to me for "correction." Naturally, a "correction" of a kind that would have satisfied them was impossible.

The second topic you mention is the interpretation of the *fall* that is proposed in *The Enigma of Evil*. It is now three years since the book's publication, and you are the first to draw attention to its new hermeneutic proposal on a subject that is so central and fundamental. The real starting point, however, of this bold hermeneutic venture was not, in my case, some a priori ambition to engage in "dialogue" with contemporary views in order to "update" theological debate. I cannot see the updating of the Church's gospel as an aim in itself, and that is why I reject "contextual" theology.

I start from the fundamental given of the apophaticism of the theological formulations. What has priority is ecclesial experience; its formulation is always relative. The "fall" constitutes an empirical conviction: an experience of the existential limits of the created—place, time, decay, death, pain, hatred, injustice. In order to identify the cause of these limits, the Church has used the relative (clearly figurative) language of the Hebrew religious tradition, the schema "commandment of God—transgression of man—punishment of transgression." Some have also extrapolated from the figurative schema a historical fact. They have thought that death entered the world after the specific event of the disobedience of the first human couple.

First, either as a historical fact or as a symbolic-figurative narrative, taking the "fall" as a consequence of disobedience becomes ensnared in a juridical understanding of God as the inflicter of a penalty and the avenger of offence given to him—an understanding radically incompatible with the triadic God of the Church, the Bridegroom and Lover of humanity. Second, it leaves not only the reality, but also the logic of the transmission, of the guilt of the first human couple to all later generations unexplained—a scandal of monstrous injustice. Third, the fact of a "fall" necessarily presupposes a prelapsarian state of created beings in which there was neither death nor decay, in which all the wild beasts only ate straw and in which roses had no thorns—a state of affairs manifestly refuted by the reality and logic of the "food chain" that from the beginning has constituted the cosmic *biocycle* of animate beings.

The *Enigma of Evil* introduces and submits to the judgment of ecclesial experience a hermeneutic proposal of "evil" that may not have ever been put together before in systematic formulation but that is clearly evident in very many aspects of the expressions of ecclesial witness: "evil" for human beings consists of the limitations (necessities) that follow from their created existence, their existential noncompleteness. Existential completeness and noncompleteness do not refer to a quantitative difference, but to a difference of *mode* of existence. Completeness of existence and life is the *mode* of freedom from any predetermination and necessity; it is the freedom of the self-causality that is realized as love, as a triadic mutual *perichōrēsis*, or interpenetration, of persons—love constitutes the existential hypostasis as rational, shared otherness, not as existential autonomous individuality.

The mode of the created is the mode of noncompleteness. It has as its cause existence outside itself, and consequently has a beginning and therefore an end. Having a beginning and an end, it has time along with finite hypostatic boundaries, that is to say, space—it exists as ontic atomicity, an atom/unit of the realization of a given *logos*, predetermined as a *mode of participation* in existence: of substance or nature. Created existence realized the *mode* of its substance or nature "with accidents," that is, with involuntary given otherness in the case of irrational existences, and with both involuntary given otherness and also the potentiality for a *mode* of willed existential otherness in the case of rational humanity. Humanity has the potentiality to exist in relative freedom from necessary predeterminations, the necessities that are imposed on it by its nature (impulses, instinct for atomic self-preservation, exercise of power, and pleasure).

It is insistence on the individualistic *mode* of the created that constitutes "evil," and freedom from this *mode*, self-transcendence in love, according to the image of the uncreated that constitutes "good." Consequently, it is not about either an inherited guilt from our forebears or a nature embodying "rebellion" against God. "Evil" is the free choice of autonomy by created existence; it is self-centeredness, self-completeness, self-love, self-eroticism, and love of pleasure.

NR: *But how does the believer access the mode of self-transcendence in love, the mode of the uncreated?* From Person and Eros *one gets the impression that it is primarily through participation in the divine energies of the triadic* perichōrēsis *through responding in* ek-stasis *to a divine summons. Others, such as Panayiotis Nellas, have spoken of participation more in terms of "Christification." What is the role of the person of Christ? How does soteriology relate to our transcending the limitations of the created?*

CY: Great care is needed in discerning the topic on which any given study is focused so as not to create misunderstandings or identity differences where they do not exist. Panayiotis Nellas focussed on the central importance that the incarnation of the Son has for the attainment of humanity's "likeness" to God. The main theme of *Person and Eros* is the clarification of the ontological content of this "likeness"—how created humanity can share in the *mode* of the uncreated as a result of the incarnation of the Logos. The one theme complements the other; it does not conflict with it. Even ecclesiastical writers who accept the historicity of the "fall" of an original human couple admit that the incarnation of the Son would have taken place even if no "fall" had preceded it—the "*theōsis*" of humanity was part of the "plan" of the divine economy for created being. Christ is the "firstborn" of the salvation "of the whole of creation," but the potentiality he inaugurated for every human being is not realized through the natural capacities of the created (the capacity for *ek-stasis*), or by means of individual moral or legal perfection, nor is it realized by any irrational "magical" (supernatural or miraculous) means. The Church's witness has a strikingly consistent ontological realism, and this realism is what *Person and Eros* explores.

Political Hesychasm

NR: *Could we turn now to the political implications of your work? A recently published book by Daniel Payne represents you as turning to fourteenth-century hesychasm for an "alternative to the modern, liberal, secular state of Greece."[8] He grants that this is not a nostalgic yearning for the past, but a concern to "instantiate the gospel in the here and now, bringing the eschaton into human experience through contemporary culture,"[9] yet he concludes you do not go far enough in separating Church from culture. How do you see the relationship between the Hellenic tradition and universal Orthodoxy? Do you accept Payne's characterization of your criticism of the modern Greek state as "political hesychasm"?*

CY: I have not yet read Daniel Payne's book and cannot conceive of what he means by the phrase "political hesychasm." This is a *contradictio in terminis*, and I am unable to understand, bearing in mind the historical facts, what relation hesychasm can have with politics in the fourteenth century, or (stranger still) with politics today.

I also find it difficult to understand why we *have* to distinguish Church from culture. Is it perhaps because we take both of these terms to refer to ideological concepts? We need to define our terms to understand each other, to offer definitions of the realities we are speaking about.

[8]Daniel P. Payne, *The Revival of Political Hesychasm in Contemporary Orthodox Thought* (Lanham, MD: Lexington Books, 2011), 234.
[9]Ibid., 264.

So, then, what is culture? Surely it is our *mode* of life: the way in which we speak (use language, exchange views), or dress, or cook, or build our houses, or decorate the spaces we occupy, or fall in love, or enjoy ourselves, or the mode of our relationships of production and exchange, and so on, and so forth. This common *mode* is differentiated, geographically and historically, because it is modeled by different collective estimations of the prioritization of human needs—which need comes first, which second, which third, and so on. But this prioritization itself arises from some "meaning" given to our existence, to the world, and to history, which most people are not aware of: What is the *cause* of the real and actually existent? What is its *goal* or *purpose*? What gives us greater joy and what less? What measures or standards justify, or do not justify, the unique existence of each one of us?

This common attribution of *meaning* that we share is clarified and expressed by talented artists, philosophers, and creative persons, in whose work most of us recognize that which empirically and in practice (as a living tradition) everybody for the most part unconsciously follows. That is why it so happens that culture is chiefly identified with the works of art, philosophy, and so on.

The Church's witness (the gospel or "good news") is also a proposition concerned with *meaning*. But it did not make its appearance historically in an intellectual or a cultural void—a fully formed mode of life and culture already existed among the peoples who were Christianized. The Greeks, specifically, had shaped a culture of a manifestly social character with characteristics that I have analyzed from many different angles in many of my books (they gave birth to the *city* and to the art of *politics*, to critical thought as a demand for the *social verification of knowledge*, to tragedy, to architecture, and to sculpture as "languages" of experiential grouping for the meaning of existent things). That is why many Fathers insist that the Greeks were "prepared in advance" to accept the Church. Their language—their means of social verification—was the only one that could *say* the ecclesial experience. Just as it is not fortuitous that Christ became incarnate from the Hebrews, so it is not at all fortuitous that the Church became incarnate from the Greeks.

The Greeks joined the Church because it offered them something they patently lacked: an *ontology* capable of shedding light on *participation in what is true* as a *causal principle* of the existential fact, that is to say, capable of identifying *existence* with *freedom* as sharing the same source. That is why the Greeks were Christianized so rapidly and of their own accord—in a time of the harsh persecution of Christians by the Roman authorities. And from this organic "encounter" of the Greeks with the Church, there was born a thousand-year civilization of astonishing achievements, a civilization that was fundamentally ecclesiocentric, to which the West would later apply the derogatory term "Byzantium."

In the post-Roman West ("The Barbarian West," in the phrase given currency by J. M. Wallace-Hadrill's classic study of that title), the Church's gospel was not chosen; it was imposed by the leaders on the primitive masses, because Christianization was at that time considered a presupposition for access to the benefits of civilization. Thus for the uncivilized nations and tribes that had invaded the West (from the fourth to the sixth century), Christianity was simply a new "religion" that came to replace (or mingle with and supplement) their pagan traditions. Western Christianity had (and continues to have to this day) all the marks of a natural religion: a predominant individualism (intellectualism, a moralistic legalism, the pursuits of individual salvation, an understanding of sin as transgression, and therefore a tormenting obsession with the guilt-redemption-justification syndrome, etc.), along with the essential loss, for the most part, of an awareness of the Church as a body in which existence and life are shared, and along with the loss of an understanding that it is the love of the communion of the saints that saves us, not our merit as individuals.

Explain to me, then, after all this, what "political hesychasm" means.

NR: *I take your point that the Greek-speaking Eastern Mediterranean was Christianized in quite a different way from the tribal Germanic world of early medieval Europe—from below, as it were, rather than from above as part of an officially imposed policy. Even when paganism was proscribed in the Eastern Empire, from the time of Theodosius II onward, the sophisticated measures taken to suppress pagan practice—the closure of temples and educational establishments only by due legal process—show that paganism no longer had a mass following. I agree that Hellenic intellectual culture—a concern to establish what is reliable and true and differentiate it from what is illusory—provided the ideal matrix for the development of Christian self-understanding. Happily, this is more acceptable now than it used to be to Western scholars, who no longer deplore (with Harnack and others) the Hellenization, as they saw it, of an originally Hebraic Christianity. The implications of this for today, however, are more controversial. Westerners often like to think they have recovered everything the Greek Fathers have to teach them and can move beyond them!*

Payne's approach is quite different, taking a sociological rather than a theological line. He sees the retrieval of a national tradition (i.e., hesychasm) as a counter to the threat of a globalized culture that is eroding a sense of national identity. I think he interprets as Byzantine "political hesychasm" the political ascendancy of hesychast patriarchs in the mid-fourteenth century under John VI Cantacouzenos, who gave their Tomoi the force of law, and as the current version of "political hesychasm" the aspiration that theological understanding should be reflected in the structure of society—creating a participatory, not authoritarian, society.

I wonder myself whether Payne's view does not reflect an interpretation of Orthodoxy—and in particular of your vision of Orthodoxy—as a "religion." I should like to explore your concept of the "religionization" of Christianity because this is, I believe, one of your most profound contributions to our understanding of the Church. How do you define a religion? How is Orthodoxy to be conceived as distinct from a religion?

CY: Before we look at Daniel Payne's views in more detail, I should like to dwell for a moment, because you go back to it yourself, on the subject of the Christianization of the tribes that invaded Western Europe from the fourth to the sixth centuries and set up states there. I press this not because history is my special field of study, but because from the whole of my work so far, I have drawn the following conclusions:

1. If we fail to appreciate, ignore, or misinterpret what happened in the western portion of the Roman Empire from the fourth to the sixth century, it becomes impossible for us to understand the medieval, and consequently the modern and contemporary, history of Europe, as well as the culture—global today—that it produced. It also becomes impossible for us to understand the schism between the Hellenized Eastern and the Latin-speaking Western (but after the tenth century completely identified with the "Franks") Church. It is impossible for us to understand ancient Greece except through the spectacles of Thomism and the "scientific" objectivity demanded by Western theology in the thirteenth century (see M.-D. Chenu, *La théologie comme science au XIII siècle*). It is impossible for us to grasp the reality of the undivided Church of the first eight centuries and the seven ecumenical councils. Western historical studies published in the last few decades have given us, with an astonishing scholarly impartiality, an exceptionally rich body of material enabling us to form a reliable picture of the historical liquidation of the Roman West and the generation and development in its place of a new world

and culture. It is therefore remarkable that even today Western societies ignore or fail to appreciate the validity of the findings of their own historians and continue to cling to ideological stereotypes of the history of the Middle Ages and the Enlightenment that belong rather to the realm of propaganda. This obstinate insistence on the bending of historical facts is characteristic of official institutional bodies representing religions and political and intellectual life in the West today—a West that leads the world in higher education.

2. The difference between the Christianization of the Greco-Roman world and that of the post-Roman West was not a difference of "manner"—by "the higher social classes" in the East, or by the "lower" in the West. It was a difference of *what* was appropriated by the East and *what* by the West. The Greek Christian literature of the first four centuries presents us with clear evidence that the Greco-Roman world appropriated the ecclesial event, that is, a new "mode of existence," whereas the then culturally more primitive West appropriated a new "religion" that it adapted to its own pagan needs and requirements. The difference is of fundamental importance (and in most respects remains so today). This does not mean that the Greco-Roman world did not also exhibit symptoms of "religionization" of the Church, especially after Theodosius the Great—the Church everywhere and at all times is a field with tares as well as wheat. The problem that historical research confirms is that in the post-Roman West of the barbarian peoples who had entered the region from outside, there was from the beginning a confusion as to what constituted the wheat and what the tares.

NR: *Scholars may differ about the precise degrees of continuity and discontinuity in the Roman provinces settled by the Germanic invaders, but nobody disputes that the barbarian world was a world of narrowing horizons and an Arian form of Christianity. It is interesting that the sorting out of the wheat from the tares was accomplished in the West by the imposition of ecclesiastical authority and the development of a clerical elite. To turn to the current situation, you have referred to the ancient Greek version of politics as a "struggle to attain truth." In Greece today, politics seems to be merely about ensuring economic survival. What is the Orthodox Church's role in this context?*

CY: Ancient Greek culture (the mode of the Hellenes) "became a preparatory instructor for Christ" not only through the philosophy, the language, and the art that it engendered, but also because it transformed the human "association for the satisfaction of needs" into a "political struggle," a struggle with a common aim so that association for the satisfaction needs (division of labor, etc.) should imitate the "*mode* of government of all things" (Heraclitus), the mode of *being true*, that is to say, the mode of *being related* "according to reason," according to "order," "harmony," and "decorum"—which are the immortal "terms," or modes, of the functioning of the universe.

The "assembly (*ecclesia*) of the people" was not simply a coming together of the citizens; it was the realization and manifestation of the *polis*, the "city": of another (new) *mode* of human existence and coexistence, a mode that aimed at *truth* and not only at satisfying utilitarian needs. With this Hellenic precedent, the first Christians defined themselves not as a "new religion" (which is always, like every religion, individualistic), but by the name of "*ecclesia*," which indicates the common struggle to realize and manifest the coexistence of the *mode* of the *true* with the mode of *becoming immortal*.

With the coming of Roman rule (from 146 BC) and the progressive Hellenization of the Roman Empire, and also during the centuries of subjection to the Turks (1453–1821), the ecclesial community (the parish-diocese) preserved the *mode* of the Greek *polis:* that a collective association, a coming together for the satisfaction of needs, should be a struggle for the realization of a mode of existence that is "in accordance with truth." In all these centuries the continuity of the social (as a political and ecclesial) struggle was preserved, not through the necessity of a particular ideological choice, but through a self-evident habituation to the continuity of this *mode*.

When the Greeks in 1821 liberated a small portion of their ancestral territory, the prevailing conditions dictated that the free Greek state should be placed under the "protection" of the then "Great Powers" of the West. These chose for the Greeks a Bavarian King (Otto Wittelsbach), who arrived in Greece with an army and advisers in order to impose the organization of what was then a modern European type of "national state." This state was, and remains to this day, unrelated to the needs, the historical habitudes, and the particular characteristics of the Greeks. Its organization, its institutions, and its functions were borrowed from contemporary (Western European) societies with a different ordering of needs, different historical habituations, and a different mentality.

For two hundred years now, the Greek state has remained a secondhand institution. Its inhabitants and citizens have not succeeded either in becoming "Europeans" or in remaining "Hellenes." As a result, they constantly slide into a decadent primitivism that somewhat resembles that of postcolonial societies, societies without their own identity and without the power to participate with a sense of their own identity and creative otherness in the historical process.

Unfortunately, in this decadent alienation of Hellenism, the Orthodox Church, not only the "autocephalous" church in the Greek state, but also the senior patriarchates of Constantinople, Alexandria, and Jerusalem, have not succeeded in playing a role in curbing it and encouraging a dynamic revival. They preceded the lay body in Westernization and alienation. They have been unable not only to exploit, but even to understand, the significance of the resistance to an alienating Westernization that was embodied in their writings by the so-called "generation of the thirties"—and before them by Papadiamantis, Spyridon Zambelios, and Ion Dragoumis. Perhaps I may be allowed, my dear Norman, to note that this is precisely the theme that I have studied for many years, and that has borne fruit in two books: *Orthodoxy and the West* and *Europe was Born from the Schism*.

* * *

CY: Let's return to Daniel Payne, now that I have read his *Revival of Political Hesychasm*. The first thing I should like to say about his book is how impressed I am by it. Although he has only read a small portion of my published work, I believe he has understood more fully than any other non-Greek scholar what I have tried to demonstrate in my writings—no Greek scholar to my knowledge has attempted anything on these lines.

Payne has understood that without a study of the philosophically very coherent, nihilistic ontology of Heidegger, I would never have become aware of the interior contradictions in the Western metaphysical (and antimetaphysical) tradition, and that consequently I would not have undertaken an investigation of the response of the Church's witness to the questions raised by ontology—the articulation of a systematic *ontology of the person*. He has understood the vital point that *apophaticism* in the Greek tradition (both ancient and Christian) constitutes an empirical social verification of knowledge that differs sharply from Western intellectualism and its "positivistic" products. He states very clearly that the ontology of the person is today a valuable gift of philosophy to political theory—a catalyst for a radical renewal of political thought and practice. He has realized at once the difference between *freedom* as an individual "right" of unrestricted choices and freedom as the achievement of breaking loose from the necessities of impersonal nature. He has understood: why the distinction between *essence* and *energy* is the only realistic basis for the refutation of the "European nihilism" proclaimed by Nietzsche; why *apophaticism* is the summit of freedom; why democracy is unattainable without a metaphysical pivot (either the Parthenon or Hagia Sophia); and why Augustine leads inexorably to Huntingdon and the NATO-inspired "New Order" of things. And so on and so forth.

Naturally, his judgments on some topics are a bit off-key. The monastic community may theoretically embody an ideal pattern of organized collectivity, a survival of the early Christian *coenobium*, but the Church's witness has never proposed it as a model of political society, if only because it is a way of life that operates as the realization of *anachōrēsis*, of withdrawal from the world. The ecclesial version or continuation of the ancient Greek *polis* could perhaps be seen as the *parish*, not the monastery. And certainly not "hesychasm," which presupposes withdrawal even from the monastic community—*hesychia* is the pursuit of the ascetic life in solitude.

Consequently, the term "political hesychasm" that Daniel Payne uses as a central theme and incorporates into the title of his work is a *contradictio in terminis*, a contradiction in both a logical and a real sense. The summary clarifications given in the book seem to me to reflect a somewhat superficial version both of politics and of hesychasm, an ideological generalization of the motives for *anachōrēsis*.

The parallel drawn between my own inquiries and those of Fr John Romanides I would also describe as somewhat superficial. I do not think that we have much in common philosophically, politically, or even ecclesiastically. In my book *Orthodoxy and the West*, I express a view, a clear view it seems to me, on this exceptionally gifted figure who wasted himself, I believe, in a fruitless, self-preservative aggressiveness. Payne's ignorance of the literature in Greek should have made him cautious when referring to Greek authors (Savvas Agouridis, Petros Vassiliadis, Hierotheos Vlachos) whom he knows only from a few of their writings or just from a single article.

If I were in Payne's position (or that of the supervisor of his doctoral studies), I would have indicated, even in the title of the thesis, which books specifically of the authors who form the subject of his study he is basing himself on, and which books he is ignoring. My own political *unease* (*an-hesychia* in Greek, not *hesychasmos*), which is strongly bound up with my philosophical inquiry and with my participation in the Church, is something I have expressed in a critical commentary on politics through a (more or less) continuous series of newspaper articles over at least forty years. These newspaper articles have all also been published as a series of books. This is perhaps why I find it puzzling that a doctoral thesis has been written on this political activity of mine, which I have tried to pursue in accordance with the criteria of the Church's witness, yet the main body of my work relevant to it has been ignored.

NR: *Yes, Payne's book, for all its merits, suffers from a lack of acquaintance with your many publications on political themes that are available only in Greek. What strikes me about the latter is their freedom from party political ideology. You attack the right and the left in Greece pretty evenhandedly, castigating a dysfunctioning state constructed in the early nineteenth century on secularist principles by the Bavarian ministers of King Otto and the disciples of Adamantios Korais. You protest at both the political preoccupations of the Orthodox Church and the privatization of religion as has occurred in Western Europe. You see yourself (pessimistically?) as defending the Thermopylae of ecclesial witness against the massed forces of indifference and secularism. How would you summarize the marks of a truly Christian society in the twenty-first century?*

CY: Both the political alignments of right, left, and center and the particular parties that express them reproduce borrowed ideologies that have been imported into Greece—not social demands and social objectives arising out of the specific needs of Greek society and serving such local needs. It is natural that not only the parliamentary political system, but also political and economic theories such as Marxism, or Keynesianism, or any other, should also have been adopted in Greece—but to serve the particularity of Greek needs, not to be motivated simply by the desire to imitate a European product, not to do it out of a sense of inferiority of the "underdeveloped" Balkans that apes whatever is "European."

My political position has always been opposed to the *secondhand* character of the state, which, as you also note, was constructed by the Bavarian commissaries of the Great Powers of the period in concert with the followers of Korais. And political life and state authority has continued in Greece, to this day, to be something foreign to the Greek and, for that reason, often inimical. They are products of theories, or perhaps practices, that are not in themselves mistaken but that at all events were generated to serve the needs of societies with different historical customs, different hierarchies of values, a different mentality, and different reflexes and manners from those of the Greeks.

Throughout the centuries, the Greeks, I believe (as I infer from my perhaps inadequate studies) have never been a "religious" people (in the sense of religion as the supreme satisfaction of instinctive psychological needs). But they have always been an intensely *metaphysical* people: it was with them that metaphysical inquiry arose, philosophy as the need to determine the *meaning* of existence, of the world, and of history—the referring phenomena to a *cause* and an *end*. Politics was one of the manifestations of this common effort to realize *the true*, along with tragedy, architecture, and sculpture. *Democracy* was not meaningful to the

Greeks without an axis of the "sacred," without the Parthenon, and later the effort of "taking part in the political process" (*politeuesthai*) was unintelligible without Hagia Sophia.

A "Christian" society is one that bases its unity and coherence not on "principles" and "regulative orders" of Christian inspiration, but on the ecclesial event that gathers living liturgical communities around the table of the Eucharist. And from this experience of communion are born art, philosophy, politics, and social institutions, as in "Byzantium."

There is not the slightest indication that something of this nature can be foreseen for the twenty-first century.

St Nikodemos the Haghiorite

NR: *At least one reviewer of* Orthodoxy and the West *was scandalized by your negative treatment of St Nikodemos the Haghiorite, whom you present as inspired by a western juridical approach to salvation. His harmonization of the canons, the* Pēdalion, *or* Rudder, *comes in for particularly severe criticism from you as a work constructed around a Western juridical emphasis on individual guilt, redemption, and justification. Other Orthodox scholars, such as John Erickson, while recognizing the limitations of Nikodemos's approach (a somewhat naive attempt to repristinate the Church by going back to earlier models, paralleling what Korais was trying to do with respect to the Greek language) nevertheless praise "his attempt to discern an inner coherence in the Church's canonical tradition" and "his refusal to see canon law as a discipline in itself, cut off from spirituality."* [10] *If Nikodemos represents a "religionization" of Christianity, as you maintain, what do you see as an acceptable alternative approach? Given that no*

---

[10]John H. Erickson, "On the Cusp of Modernity: The Canonical Hermeneutic of St Nikodemos the Haghiorite (1748–1809)," *St Vladimir's Theological Quarterly* 42.1 (1998): 45–66.

society can exist without some kind of regulative framework,
how should the Church appropriate its canonical tradition?

CY: I think that it was not just one reader who was scandalized
by my presentation of the work of Nikodemos in *Orthodoxy*
and the West. There were more. In my opinion—and I may be
wrong—those who were scandalized were readers who had
(consciously or unconsciously) appropriated a Roman Catholic
version of "holiness": its identification with "infallibility" and
"sinlessness." But I must insist that the Church does not idolize
either "truths" or persons. The Church does not construct idols
out of knowledge or virtue. In the persons of the saints, it recognizes the first fruits of the "kingdom": created beings who have
been vouchsafed by God to act as instruments of the outpouring
and manifestation of his love, to exist as beings that love and
are loved. Unfortunately, the process too of the proclamation of
the saints seems historically to have been influenced by Roman
Catholic legalism.

The holiness of Nikodemos the Haghiorite does not negate
the fact that Nikodemos was a child of his age, nor is his holiness impaired by the inevitable historical influences to which he
was subjected. Of course, I am not acquainted with the thinking of the standing synod of the Patriarchate of Constantinople
that led to Nikodemos being declared a saint—whether he was
canonized because in the popular mind he was acknowledged as
"teeming with rivers of miracles," like St Nektarios, for example,
or because he was recognized as a "Father," as a teacher of the
ecclesial body.

If he was proclaimed a saint as a "Father," in the sense that
Paul gives to the word (1 Cor 4.15), then I am entitled to "tell the
Church" (Mt 18.17) of my own "scandalization." This is presupposed as a question in the book we are discussing: Is the juridical,
legal relationship of humankind with God, not as a figurative
expression or illustrative form of words, but as a hermeneutic

proposition determinative of the kind of relation (a proposition that shapes and expresses the mind of the Church), compatible with ecclesial experience and (evangelical) witness?

Can Anselm of Canterbury's theory that Christ was crucified so that the righteousness of God the Father that was offended by human disobedience should receive "satisfaction," a theory that St Nikodemos adopts without reservation, prove acceptable to the Church's conscience? Does it have the slightest connection with what the Church sees in Christ's death on the cross?

I would ask you to take everything said in *Orthodoxy and the West* about the legalistic ethics of St Nikodemos and his codification of moral rules (chiefly in the *Chrēstoētheia* and the *Pēdalion*) as questions, because that is how they are meant. They are questions that presuppose the fact that holiness within the Church is not to be inferred either from the correctness of theoretical views or from the linguistic coherence of their expression—as a gift of a different order, it can therefore coexist with elements that in a specific historical period and in particular circumstances constituted the dominant "Christian" outlook, even though they stood in manifest contradiction to the Church's gospel.

At any rate, allow me to observe that I do not "attribute" the adoption of Western legalism to St Nikodemos (such a charge seriously distorts my view), but I infer it from his work and give precise references. This carefully documented demonstration cannot be described as "particularly severe criticism" by me of his work. Moreover, I am unable to comprehend such nebulous expressions (at the opposite pole from linguistic coherence and seriousness) as those of John Erickson about Nikodemos's "naive attempt to repristinate the Church by going back" (by legalism, juridicism, and the psychopathological inflation of a sense of guilt!) "to earlier models" or about an "inner coherence" (!) "in the Church's canonical tradition" where "spirituality" (what in fact does this overused word mean?) has priority.

The generation of the Church's canons, the formation of the "canonical" tradition, and later its misinterpretation and distortion are matters that have been analyzed (by me, at least, in *The Freedom of Morality*), and I have nothing further to add. Paul describes the "law" as a *curse* (Gal 3.10, 13), a means of armorplating the ego, an exclusion from the *salvation* that is our participation in, and appropriation of, the communion of love, which is the Church: a charismatic realization of the existential freedom of the Uncreated. The canons can only have a pedagogical character, a character that indicates to us how far we are from the ecclesial mode of existence on account of our self-sufficiency, our egocentrism.

I believe, my dear Norman, perhaps mistakenly, that if, against all hope, God granted the Church today the Eighth Ecumenical Council that we have been awaiting for thirteen centuries, in the midst of the tremendous confusion following the schism, the Reformation, and the splitting apart of the much-fragmented reformed "confessions," the theme of the council could be (or it would suffice it to be) a single one above: Is the salvation proclaimed by Christian witness an individual or an ecclesial event? Is it a reward according to the merits of the individual (*axiomisthia*), or is it a charism of participation, of communion, given as a response (*antidorēma*) to the freedom of human beings to wish to exist only in order to be loved and to love?

Please read and judge the work of St Nikodemos the Haghiorite. Does it refer to salvation as an individual event, the attaining of a reward centered on the self, which is supported by the ecclesiastical institution and the way it functions? Or does it identify salvation with the gift of participation in the ascetic endeavor of realizing the triadic mode of existence?

Salvation is not something added to our otherwise complete human nature as transformable in freeing us from the bounds of finitude...

Ecclesial Experience

Salvation and *Theōsis*

NR: *Your vision of salvation as freedom from the bounds of fini-tude is central to your thinking. It utterly transcends any notion of salvation understood as something added to our otherwise complete human nature, let alone a version of salvation that is merely moralistic. One criticism I have heard expressed, though, which I should like to ask you to clarify, is that the language of* ek-stasis, *which you use notably in* Person and Eros, *seems to imply that by passing from the mode of the created to the mode of the uncreated, we leave our nature behind and, in effect, cease to be human. Surely this is a mistaken impression?*

CY: These reservations about the term "*ek-stasis*" arise, I think from a mistaken understanding of the term "nature" or "essence." Nature/essence is understood as *some-thing*, as an onticity defined in itself with attributes and qualities. Perhaps it is not fully appre-ciated that in the Greeks' linguistic code these words (both of them) always signified not an objective *what* but an active *how*: a *mode* of existence, the *common* mode of each species of exis-tents. The word "essence" (*ousia*, derived from the feminine of the present participle of the verb "to be," *einai*) indicates the *mode of participation* in being, and the word "nature" (*physis*, from the verb *phyomai*, "I shoot forth," "I grow") indicates existence as becoming, that is, again as a *mode*, not as a static state.

95

nature/essence in Greek is not an objective __what__ but an active __how__

So when we speak of the essence or nature of God, we mean the *mode* of the *uncreated*, a mode of the self-cause of existence, of freedom from any necessity imposed by existence, a mode of *free will* for existence that realizes existence as *love*. The hypostasis of the *Father* (a *personal* hypostasis, that is, a hypostasis that exists and is manifested only as an event of loving/free *relation:* "generating" the Son and causing the Spirit to "proceed") has precedence (nontemporally and lovingly). The names of all three hypostases of the thearchic Triad—"Father," "Son," and "Spirit"—indicate the existence and manifestation of existence, as events of loving *relation*, that is, of free will for existence: They exist not because their existence is a given, predetermined necessity; they do not simply manage their obligatory existence. They exist because they will to exist, and they will to exist because they love. They *hypostasize* their *being*—they make their existence hypostatic or real—as an event of relation/communion of existence; they realize and manifest their *being* as a mode of *freedom*, a mode of love.

God "stands out" (*existatai*) from this *mode* of existence of the uncreated by means of the incarnation of the Son/Logos. He who exists not through necessity, but by his free will, becomes incarnate, that is, exists by the mode of the necessity of existence that characterizes the created. He exists as finite atomicity, subject to impersonal natural needs (for food, drink, and sleep; the circumscription of time and space) and even to death.

This assumption of the mode of createdness, however, this *ek-stasis* from the mode of the uncreated, is voluntary; it takes place freely "through a superabundance of love." That is, it takes place by the mode of the uncreated. Incarnate, the Son does not abandon the *mode* (essence/nature) of the uncreated; he does not transform his essence/nature. Because the mode of his uncreated existence is the freedom of love, he also assumes out of the freedom of love the *mode* of the created—Christ becomes the first *theōsis in granted as gift, but acquired as a possession*

human being (the firstborn of a new creation) who, even though
he is earthly, exists because he wills to exist, and he wills to exist
because he loves. He loves the clay that he has assumed (he sets
that clay on the throne/mode of Godhead), but he wills to exist as
a human being primarily (*timelessly*) because he loves the Father
and "does" (incarnates) as man "the will of the Father who sent
me," that is, the participation of the created in the mode of existence of the uncreated (cf. Jn 6.39–40).

The mode of the uncreated is freedom from any existential predetermination, and therefore the free *ek-stasis* from this mode—
the voluntary, loving assumption of the limitations of createdness
(even until death, "the death of the cross")—is the affirmation
of the existential freedom of God, an affirmation that "God is
love" (1 Jn 4.16). The Son's incarnation breaks down "the wall
of partition" that by definition separated the uncreated from the
created and "inaugurates" the path of the *theōsis* of the created.
Linguistically "*theōsis*" too can be defined only as *ek-stasis*: the
appropriation of the *mode* of existence of the uncreated, without
identification with that mode, without extinguishing the original
difference of the created. This appropriation is granted by grace;
it is not acquired through the inherent powers of the created.

The language of ecclesial experience dares to speak of the
"*theōsis*," or deification, of the created: a path inaugurated by the
Son through his incarnation, death, and resurrection. He inaugurates it as a gift of grace, a charism that is granted from God's love
(a love free from any existential limitation) to the freedom of the
human person. *Theōsis* is granted as a gift; it is not acquired as a
possession. Created nature exists with its createdness as an insu-
perable existential boundary. It cannot of itself exist in the mode
of the uncreated, nor can the mode of the uncreated be imposed
by force, destroying the freedom of the personal ("in the image
of God") *mode* of its existence.

More specifically, the "imitation of Christ" is not sufficient for the *theōsis* of the human person. It is not enough that people should imitate the *kenōsis* of the Son (his humiliation, self-denial, sacrificial self-offering) in order to achieve freedom from the bounds of createdness. Freedom from nature in the sense of the *ek-stasis* achieved by a *fakir* or by a Christian monk who approaches the ascetic life in a spirit of athletic competitiveness is one thing; the realization of the existence (hypostasis) of the created when *participation* in the *mode* of the uncreated is granted to it (as a gift of grace/charism of divine life-giving love) is another. Our goal is *ek-stasis* and *theōsis*, not simply in relation to certain necessities entailed by createdness, but *ek-stasis* from the mode of the created to the mode of true life granted by grace and received in freedom and love. *Theōsis* is bestowed in return on the freedom of the created person, a freedom that can be realized existentially in the ecclesial struggle of the ascetic life, and also in the "Remember me" of the robber's repentance at the point of death.

NR: *The term* "theōsis" *has become rather fashionable recently in Anglophone theological discourse, but it is often understood in individualistic terms, as an egocentric quest for salvation. How would you describe our participation in the divine life? Is a divine mode of existence attainable only eschatologically?*

CY: If I understand it correctly, the word "*theōsis*" in the language of the Church does not mean the addition in a "miraculous" (ontologically inexplicable) way of some divine "properties" to a created, mortal human being. The difference between man and God is not exhausted in individually negotiated "properties," but in the differentiation of the *mode of existence*.

There is the *mode* of the uncreated Causal Principle of existence and of that which exists, and there is the *mode* of createdness, the mode of that which has been caused by the First Cause (the First Cause's results). The *theōsis* of human beings means that even though human beings are created, they may exist not in the *mode* of the created (the caused), but in the *mode* of the uncreated (the Cause).

The fundamental createdness of human beings is not annulled by their *theōsis*—human beings remain created existences, because the Cause of the fact that they exist is not connected with their own will and decision. But the power of human beings to be free from the *mode* (the limitations) of createdness also belongs (as a possibility) to human nature. It belongs to the *personal* mode of their existence—to their power of refusing the impersonal, instinctual needs of their nature. This power of human beings to exist as free (up to a point) from the existential needs imposed by createdness is described in the Church's language as humanity's gift of having been created "in the image of God."

Freedom is the reality and the measure that differentiates the *mode* of the uncreated from the *mode* of the created. But in the case of this difference, we are not speaking about freedom as the unimpeded power of making individual choices. We are speaking about *existential* freedom, the power of detachment/liberation from the necessities that accompany createdness.

Created beings did not choose to exist. The *mode* of the created is subjection to necessity. The existence of created beings has a beginning and an end. The passage from our given beginning to our inexorable end is a continuous and progressive *ek-stasis* (a "standing-outside-of," the etymological root of the English word "ecstasy") from existing, a gradual exist from existing, an *ek-stasis* that is realized as *decay* and is experienced/measured as *time*.

Time and space, decay and death, are not results of some sinful *fall* that followed the creation of humanity. They are the given limitations that distinguish the created from the uncreated. If humanity had been created immortal and uncircumscribed, we would not have been human. We would not have been creatures/

creations of God but *consubstantial* with God (with the same *mode* of existence)—we would have had to have been "begotten" by the Father, like the Son; or caused to "proceed," like the Spirit.

The *mode* of the uncreated is freedom without predeterminations or limitations. This freedom is summarized by ecclesial experience in the word "father." Ecclesial experience acknowledges the Cause of existence and of that which exists not as *God*, but as *Father*. The word "God" reveals an existence that is predetermined (by its "divine" nature or *essence*) to be that which it is (timeless, uncircumscribed, all-powerful, all-wise, etc.)—an existence that cannot not be that which it is, nor can it exist by a mode other than that of Godhead. So by the rationale of *essence*, God is obliged to be that which he is. Consequently, the Causal Principle of *being* (of existence and of that which exists) is an inexplicably given necessity—it is not freedom.

Ecclesial experience recognizes the Cause of *being* as a rational existence (an existence that is self-conscious and active, capable of relations, and creative of relations) that is free from any existential predetermination, from any necessity of a given nature or essence. The Cause of *being* exists because it freely *wills* to exist, and it wills to exist because it *loves*. Love is not a "property" of the Causal Principle; it is its nature/essence, that is to say, its *mode* of existence the mode of freedom, of nonsubjection to any ulterior motive of freedom.

All these linguistic definitions of love, as embodying freedom and the creative Causal Principle of existence and of that which exists, are summed up in the word "Father." The Church's experience uses it to indicate the hypostatic realization of existence as relation, as self-transcendence and self-offering. The word does not refer to a primordial, existential individuality (a being that is supreme, divine, of the most honorable kind) that subsequently appropriates fatherhood; it refers to an existence that exists *because* (insofar as and provided that) it "begets" the Son and causes the Spirit to "proceed." Fatherhood is the hypostatic character of the Causal Principle of that which exists, the given that makes it a hypostasis, a real existence. The Causal Principle does not exist at the beginning and subsequently "begets" and "causes to proceed"; it exists *because* it "begets" and "causes to proceed." The definitive (and defining) character of the Causal Principle, the *mode* of its existence, its nature/essence, is love. The only definition of God in the Church's gospel is that "God is love" (1 Jn 4.9, 16). God does not "have" love. The word does not refer to the way God conducts himself, to his operations *ad extra* (his relations with what is external to him). Love refers to that which God *is*, to the mode of his existence.

All three words, "Father," "Son," and "Spirit," are astonishingly original linguistic usages designed to signify/define *personal* (hypostatic) realizations of *being* that are free from any presupposed ontic individuality. Each person of the thearchic Triad *is* (exists and is known) not in itself but *as-toward*. The relation/love toward the Son and the Spirit constitutes and manifests the Father; the relation/love toward the Father and the Spirit constitutes and manifests the Son; the relation/love toward the Father and the Son constitutes and manifests the Spirit.

The person of the Son and *Logos* (with the word "*Logos*" signifying the manifestation/making-known of the Godhead), free from any limitation/predetermination of *essence* or *nature*, is also free to exist in the *mode* of created/mortal humanity (through love alone, which also constitutes him as a hypostasis). He assumes the limitations and necessities of createdness in the hypostatic freedom of his loving sonship, and by this assumption (the *incarnation* of the Son) makes their abolition an existential reality. The limitations lose their limiting character, and the necessities lose their inexorable character. The incarnation of the *Logos* embodies (actualizes, or turns into an existential reality, a *mode* of existence) the transformation of createdness into freedom. And the *mode* of the transformation is that of the thearchic Triad: *love*.

Just as the Son exists not as a self-subsistent entity, but because he is loved by the Father and loves the Father, so too by the assumption (through the superabundance of loving goodness) of createdness/humanity by the Son, every created/mortal human being can henceforth exist free from any existential limitation, thanks to the same love by which the Father hypostasizes the Son. Every human being becomes *a son of the Father by grace*; it is sufficient for him or her, through letting go of self and self-offering, to embody Christ's *"Amen"*: a free, loving consent to adoption by the Father.

The *theōsis* of human beings that ecclesial experience speaks of is thus synonymous with their *salvation*. Human beings are "saved" (become safe/whole, and even though created, attain to the wholeness/integrity of existence and of life); they attain the "likeness" to God that was the potential goal of their creation in God's image. In the words of Gregory of Nyssa, "Man goes out of his own nature, having become immortal out of mortality, pure out of impurity, eternal out of impermanence, and wholly god out of his human state" (*On the Beatitudes* 7 [PG 44:1280C–D]). Or as Maximus the Confessor expresses it, "That we should come to be wholly of God alone, reflecting the divine radiance in all the movements of our soul and body. And to put it simply, let us become receptive of the whole of God and altogether wholly gods by grace, without becoming identical to him with regard to essence" (*Letter* 1 [PG 91:376A–B]).

What *saves* human beings and *deifies* them is not their individual ethical achievements, their feats of individual virtue, their heroic asceticism, or their preeminence in the struggle against the flesh. What *saves* and *deifies* them is participation in the Church, in the *mode* of the Church (the ecclesial community). The *mode* of the Church is the *mode* of Christ, who enfleshed (made the *mode* of humanity) the *mode* of triadic love: that human beings too should exist by drawing their existence not from their *nature*, which is subject to necessities, but should exist because they love and are loved. The salvation/deification of a human being is not an achievement of the individual; it is an ecclesial gift. With the Church a human being realizes the *mode* of Christ, the making flesh of the *mode* of triadic love.

We are saved because we are loved by Christ, our bridegroom-lover; by the all-holy mother of God; and by the saints of the Church—this concentrated storm of love hypostasizes (makes a real existence of) all human beings who freely and actively give their assent, the "amen" of their self-abandonment, to the loving ecclesial community of people of the same kind.

Consequently, the salvation/*theōsis* that we look for is not unlimited survival as individuals, but the *wholeness* (the *plērōma*, or fullness) of every loving relation that, in the mode of the created, we live in a fragmentary, deficient way. If even upon earth, bound as we are to necessity, we sense something of the wonder of love; the radiance of beauty; the exhilaration of creation and innovation; the joy of having children; the delight of sharing our existence with another, of giving our body in marriage, of tasting the limitlessness of personal otherness in the expressiveness of art—if all these things make existence thrilling even though subject to decay and death, what we await "in hope" is their *completion* and *fulfillment*: "What no eye has seen, nor ear heard, nor the human heart conceived, what God has prepared for those who love him" (1 Cor 2.9).

NR: *I agree that the vast majority of people who identify them-selves as Christians take it for granted that salvation is individual. Chenu and others are undoubtedly right in connecting this indi-vidualistic approach with the rise of the universities in twelfth-century Europe, when intellectualism came to dominate Western*

Christianity. The autonomy of the intellect that was thus brought about meant that salvation was seen as something added to the human person as a gratuitous gift of grace. As such, salvation could not be an ontological transformation of the human person; it could not be deification. Salvation in terms of deification is not just a matter of the will, however much assisted by grace, nor is it simply an eschatological state to be enjoyed on the basis of individual merit.

There are strong indications that many Western Christians are no longer satisfied with such an account of salvation. Henri de Lubac, for example, wanted to see salvation as a participatory putting on of the divine nature. He saw that otherwise it would be a purely nominal change mediated by the power structures of the Church. Recently, some Reformed theologians, attracted by Orthodoxy's teaching on theōsis, *have been turning away from the forensic concept of justification and exploring a more trans-formatory model. But their idea of salvation is still individualistic rather than communitarian. The sense of ourselves as autono-mous individuals is so difficult to overcome. How do you envis-age a communitarian version of salvation that nevertheless still allows for the continuing identity of the human person?*

CY: You touch on a very important question that allows us again to make explicit the specific experience that characterizes the Church's witness. Intellectualism is a stage or phase of human-ity's immaturity; it belongs to the period of its youth, a period in which humanity needs the protective security of "objective" certainties. Humanity wants to possess knowledge on an indi-vidual or atomic basis, and its intellectual capacity offers it the impression that it possesses it by identifying "certain" knowledge with the signifiers that (subject to intellectual definition) define comprehension.

The West, in its youthful enthusiasm or youthful immaturity, identified (and still identifies) the *comprehension* of the signifiers with the *knowledge* of what is signified. It accepted and cultivated an "ontic" version of being, as Heidegger very astutely evinced. That is, the West saw being always as onticity, brought to accomplishment and objectively defined with a sense of finality by the individual intellect (the *adaequatio rei et intellectus* defines and exhausts the *truth*, the *veritas*, of reality's every given).

And in an "ontic" onticity (an onticity that is intellectually defined and objective), that which the Church calls *salvation* or *grace* can only be understood as the addition of "objective" properties, capacities, or attributes—a quantitative addition, since that which is added is also objectively defined. But an existential addition to that which is a definitively completed existent, to the *natural* (to that which is defined by the intellectual definition of its *nature* or its *essence*), can only be an extra-natural, that is, *super-natural*, thaumaturgic-magical given—something like an indeterminate power or "energy," a "gift" of existential capacities allegorically termed "grace" or "salvation."

By contrast, the Church always understood being in terms of *mode*, that is, as an event, as a dynamic becoming and not as a definitively accomplished onticity. *Nature* or *essence* is the common *mode* of the uniformity of species (*homoeideia*) of existent things, and *hypostasis* is also a *mode*, the unique dissimilar and unrepeatable mode of every partial existent. Every existent hypostasis of whatever nature or essence possesses a modal, or at least a modal otherness, or at least an otherness of outward form (*morphē*). Only the rational hypostasis of every human being also possesses, beyond its formal, or morphic, otherness, an otherness that is actively realized, an otherness with regard to the common (and consequently necessary for every partial hypostasis) characteristics of the nature or essence. The common characteristics of the fact of existing constitute a given existential necessity. The active (willed) otherness we can exercise with regard to the necessities of the common nature constitutes the possibility of human *freedom*.

Essence or nature is a *mode*. Hypostasis is also a *mode*. The mode is *activated* (*energeitai*) or realized existentially, through activities (*energēmata*); it is not objectified statically through being defined by the intellect. And it is activated either in a pre-determined fashion (by the given nature or essence of the existent) or in an indeterminate fashion when it has to do with the causal principle of the fact of existing, existence as self-cause. The activated *mode* is always reason (*logos*), that is, a manifestation of existence in action (*en-ergē*), a manifestation of nature activated in a specific hypostasis of nature or essence.

The Church recognizes and bears witness to (proclaims) two *modes* of being: the mode of the *created* and the mode of the *uncreated*. The created has the cause of its being outside of itself; the reason-mode, the *logos-tropos* (nature or essence), of the being of every created entity is a given, a necessary presupposition of its participation in existence. The created does not choose freely to exist or not to exist. Existence is a necessity for the created. We realize existence as an innate, autonomous urge or necessity for existence: an urge for self-preservation, for the imposition of power, for pleasure. Every individual hypostasis of the realm of the existent realizes existence as an end in itself. It realizes existence independently of its will, as a given necessity.

Submission to existence as a necessity that is an end in itself, necessity of our instincts, our urges and our passions, is realized in every partial created hypostasis as an active *mode* of atomic (and individualistic) existential autonomy: the individual of every living species survives by putting to death individuals of other species (of the plant or animal kingdom) in order to nourish itself, and the same individual will also be put to death at some time so that other species (microbes, bacilli, bacteria, etc) will also be preserved. We call this phenomenon *the food chain*. This submission to existence as a necessity that is an end in itself, terminating inexorably in the death of every created individuality, we speak of as a *fall*, that is, as a reduction from a fuller to a lesser *mode* of existence. In fact, what we are referring to is the difference between the *mode* of the created and the *mode* of the uncreated.

The created exists in the *mode* of necessity, the uncreated in the *mode* of freedom, freedom from any kind of necessity whatsoever. This same uncreated is the cause of its own existence; there is not some logic or some necessity that compels it to exist. It exists because it wants to exist, and it wants to exist because it loves. Love is the summit of freedom, the guarantee of freedom—it is impossible for you to love by necessity. The *mode* of the uncreated is love, that is, the fullness of freedom, and it is the mode of existence and action. In our human language, the *mode* by which we signify the uncreated as the self-conscious, rational freedom of love, as the self-cause of existence and the cause of every existent thing, is the word "Father": he who freely wills to exist, who wills it because he loves. And he hypostasizes his love in an existential event: he "begets" the Son timelessly and lovingly, and he causes the Spirit to "proceed." He realizes existence as freedom from existence, as a kenotic self-emptying from every demand of self-existence, as the triadic/loving *perichōrēsis*, or mutual indwelling, of existence.

The West rejects the distinction between *essence* and the *energies* of the essence and opposes St Gregory Palamas (thinking that the distinction compromises the "simplicity" of God!), precisely because it insists on an ontic-noetic definition of essence or substance. The West is unaware that the essence is a *mode*, that the *mode* simply becomes active (*energeitai*), and that it is active without the activity (*energeia*, or "energy") replacing or annihilating the identity of the one acting.

The hope of the Church, its gospel, is that through death the human person enters into the "kingdom" that has been "prepared" by Christ, the incarnate Son, the "kingdom" that is the timelessness of freedom from the bounds of createdness. We shall exist not by necessity, but because we shall want to exist, and we shall want to exist because we shall love. If we do not want it, we shall not exist. A mind-reeling freedom, intoxication, and rapture of love.

NR: *Fr Andrew Louth has recently drawn attention to the realism of your analysis of love, noting that your* Variations on the Song of Songs *begins strikingly with the statement, "We come to know love only in the context of failure." Elsewhere you have written of marriage as a "tough confrontation of egos" that involves rows, bitter words, and the wounding of feelings. Whatever success we have in learning not to impose our own will on our partner, "the price paid in pain banishes any sense of achievement." You imply that nevertheless it is the human experience of sharing, of withdrawing from the autonomy of the ego, that enables us to mirror the kenotic self-denial of Christ and thus make the transition to a divine mode of existence possible. How would you characterize the transition to such a mode of existence in terms as equally realistic as those you have used for marriage?*

CY: I would remind you, Norman, of the astonishing saying of St Maximus the Confessor: "Without desire there is no yearning, the end of which is love." I think that Maximus is using the word "desire" (*epithymia*) in the sense which we give it today in the post-Freudian age: it is an impersonal instinctive urge, an urge to appropriate, dominate, and possess the "other" opposite us, with the aim of securing individual pleasure. It is a necessity of nature.

"Yearning" (*pothos*) is the experience of desire but in a way that has been made personal: we desire a specific "other"; our desire refers to the difference of the "other." What attracts us, arouses us, elates us, is not just any desirable object, but some or all of the unique, dissimilar, and unrepeatable marks of a specific "other." Despite its reference to the *rational* (manifestatory of reason) reality of the other, and perhaps also to the other's *personal* active difference, yearning is linked rather to the instinctual (bound up with natural necessity) character of desire. That is why it so often happens that although we are absolutely sure that we have fallen "wholly" and "forever" in love with a particular person, only the passage of some time is needed for us to "discover" that our certainties were merely an illusion.

St Maximus tells us, if I am interpreting him correctly, that the aim, the goal (the "end"), of yearning is love (*agapē*). Love means to come out of my egoistic self, to free myself from the natural self-interest of the urge, in order to admit the other as a participant in my live and existence, to share life and existence with the "other," which means my will, my perspectives, and my natural urges and desires. It means that the "other" should become for me the presupposition and potentiality of my renouncing my existential atomicity and self-interest. It means that my whole existence should be love "in the likeness" of the existence of God.

And this miracle should be accomplished "imperceptibly," without the slightest awareness that we are aiming at a reward. Freedom should be attained by the *mode* of createdness through the humble acceptance of the necessities of createdness. Thus *desire* and *yearning* are manifested as elements of the creation of humanity "in the image of God," elements with which the nature of humanity, of every human being, was endowed. The "power to love," the main element of being "in the image," is sown in human nature—"as if a man should scatter seed upon the ground, and should sleep and rise night and day, and the seed should sprout and grow, he knows not how" (Mk 4.26–28).

Of course, love does not cease to be a potentiality—not a necessity as desire and yearning are, but a potentiality that (I would be so bold to say) *nature* "offers" to the *person*, through desire and yearning. Freedom exploits desire and yearning in order to attain kenotic love, to realize by eros for bodies the eros of Christ for the Church.

St Maximus' saying radically overturns the fear of sexuality that (in a silent but tormenting fashion) is innate in the religious person. I would say that Maximus completes Paul's thesis on the realization, through sexual relations, of the mutual self-giving and self-offering which makes marriage a "mystery" (or "sacrament"), that is, a manifestation of the Church, of the *mode* of the kingdom. Unfortunately, the religionization of the ecclesial event has rendered sexuality guilty by definition in the conscience of a large part of the Christian and non-Christian population. The incompatibility of priesthood with sexuality in Roman Catholicism, and the prohibition of a second marriage for widower clerics in "Orthodoxism," are among the more inhuman manifestations of the religious version of sexuality as "pollution" and "impurity."

Clerical Celibacy and Monastic Life

NR: *You have written critically in several places about monks—or rather, about the dangers of monastic élitism, an élitism that you see as connected with a fear of sexuality or severe feelings of guilt about sex. (In some ways you remind me of the much maligned Jovinian, who in the fourth century protested at the elevation of celibacy above marriage in the teaching of certain ascetics, such as Jerome, on the grounds that it undermined the value of baptism, and who was condemned for his pains by Ambrose of Milan and Pope Siricius!) Monks like St Silouan the Athonite, who never had any ambition to become a great staretz but lived in a state of profound humility, clearly do not come under your stricture. But* *you do regard the choice of celibacy by nonmonastic clergy in the Orthodox Church as highly undesirable, don't you?*

CY: In my many writings in different genres there is not a single negative reference, I believe, to the Church's asceticism and monasticism, for I have a deep respect, and in some cases awe, for those who achieve it. There is a text dating from my youth, a poetic, imaginative fable, "Niphon the Kelliote," published in *Hunger and Thirst*, that still expresses my feelings.

Last year I wrote another small piece, "In Praise of Marriage," and I imagine that this is what you are referring to. In this article I compare marriage with monasticism, not in order to depreciate monasticism, but to record one tiny protest against the constant flagrant disparagement of marriage.

The whole of ecclesial life is distorted and alienated when it is religionized, when the witness of ecclesial experience—the good news of the gospel—is construed as an ideology; faith, as an individual's conviction; and morality, as a meritorious individual achievement. In the context of monasticism, such distortion becomes much more emphatic, producing lamentable symptoms of unhealthy religious obsession and a delusion that torments its victims.

In my personal, perhaps mistaken, judgment, monasticism today, in the churches that call themselves the Orthodox, manifests two pernicious symptoms. The first you have touched on in your question: it is a celibacy that has been made independent of monastic life and monastic *anachōrēsis* or withdrawal, a celibacy that is lived without membership of and participation in a spiritual community/brotherhood/family, without *anachōrēsis* and the eremitical life. Celibacy is chosen only as the presupposition for a career, since synodically and canonically it has been applied only to bishops.

Celibacy cut off from monastic life, as the prerequisite of an episcopal career, automatically devalues sexuality. It stigmatizes it and renders it guilty, since axiomatically it excludes even the most holy of the married clergy from episcopal responsibility. The compulsory celibacy of the episcopate proves all that the bishops preach at the same time about marriage as a *mystery* "for Christ and for the Church" to be hypocritical blather. If a "mystery" really does signify the realization and manifestation of the Church, that is, the existential *mode* that images the Trinity and the *kenōsis* of the Son, how is it possible that the *mystery* of marriage should not exclude from the first and second grades of priesthood but should exclude from the third grade (!) or that the "indelible" charism of priesthood should forbid the mystery of (a second) marriage of priests who have become widowers!

In today's conditions of a "modern" society, celibacy, as the institutionalized prerequisite of an episcopal career, presents an extreme risk to the mental health and moral integrity of whoever ventures upon it. Loneliness in modern large cities literally ruins the celibate who is not part of a monastic community. His unavoidable participation in modern conditions of life (parties, television, video, internet, etc., with the constant bombardment of provocations to indulge in sensual pleasure that these entail) leads inexorably to the maximizing of possible psychological disorder, sexual perversion, and neurotic or psychotic disturbance. Or else the conditions of the celibate's secular life encourage him to resort to double standards; to systematic hypocrisy; and to schizoid, contradictory forms of behavior.

NR: *This is a problem that has devastated the Roman Catholic Church since it came to light in the 1990s.*

CY: Yes, the frightful scandals concerning pederasty that for decades now have rocked the Roman Catholic clergy, or, among the same clergy, the silently condoned illicit marriages—chiefly in Latin America and Africa—with women who are hidden away like sex slaves without any part in society, are characteristic aspects of the tragedy that perpetuates a primeval attitude of guilty fear and a psychopathological repugnance toward sexuality as a supposedly "Christian" stance. But in the "national" churches of the confessional form of Orthodoxy that I call "Orthodoxism," we have similar problems: the high degree of psychopathology, of lamentable human immaturity, and of pernicious detachment from the spirituality both of the Church and of the world evident in episcopal bodies and the "courts" that surround them hits you in the face.

Of course, even the celibacy that is practiced in a monastic community can easily become the basis for the career of a "spiritual public prosecutor" when the ecclesial event is religionized. The Church of Greece, at any rate, has suffered this ordeal for several decades now. Simple monks, with the "authority" that they think their monastic dress and their living in a monastery guarantees them, constantly and provocatively pop up in public life as infallible spokesmen for "genuine" Christian teaching. They judge and condemn patriarchs, archbishops, and synods for "concessionism" with regard to faith and the falsification of doctrines—they believe themselves to stand in the tradition of John Chrysostom and Mark Eugenikos. They even go so far as to celebrate the Eucharist without commemorating the bishop, with the absolute certainty that they possess the "truth," the integral Orthodox faith.

Many Orthodox churches live under the reign of terror of these overbearing "zealots," monks who operate as censors and public prosecutors, tormenting the body of the Church. It would not be an exaggeration to claim that they compensate for their sexual sterility by the pleasure—much more intoxicating for the ego—of the "metaphysical" authority that the monastic habit gives them.

The Theological Challenges of the Twenty-First Century

NR: *Your hopes that an eighth ecumenical council might focus on the subject of salvation, clarifying whether this is fundamentally an individual or an ecclesial event, raises fascinating questions. Metropolitan Kallistos (Ware) has expressed the conviction that if the contribution of Orthodox thinkers to theological discourse in the twentieth century has been in the field of ecclesiology, in the present century it will be in the field of anthropology. There seems to be a similar feeling in the West about the way theology is moving. One author, Daniel Helminiak, has recently written, "No longer are revelation, God, and religious belief the starting points of theology. Rather, the foundation of theology, and of all human endeavors, is the human spirit and its requisite authenticity."[1] What do you see as the principal theological challenges of the twenty-first century?*

CY: Is it possible that a person as attractive and intelligent as Fr Kallistos Ware should believe that the "theological dialogue" of the twentieth century (which unfortunately still continues) interests anyone beyond those pursuing a professional career in religious institutions? Does this dialogue have the slightest relation to the needs, the anxieties, and the perplexities of people today, with their thirst for the *meaning* of life and existence? Does this dialogue produce any propositions or any testimony concerning our experiential groping for *meaning*? Does it produce any art? Does it have any repercussions on the way we understand politics or social institutions? Does it at least influence, even in the slightest degree, our intellectual life and the issues it grapples with? Let us not deceive ourselves. This is a "dialogue" between political institutions of religious authority that concerns only the bureaucrats preoccupied with institutional interests.

---

[1]Daniel Helminiak, "Spirituality as an Explanatory and Normative Science," *The Heythrop Journal* 52.4 (July 2011): 596–627.

As far as your quotation from Helminiak is concerned, forgive me if I find it utterly puerile. What does "the human spirit" mean? What ontological reality is defined by this phrase? And how do we measure the "authenticity" of the human spirit"? When is this abstract notion of "the human spirit" "authentic" and when is it "nonauthentic"? And if the "foundation" of theology is not the historical experience of revelation, the experiential verification of the Causal Principle of that which exists as a possibility of *relation* (of faith/trust) with the personal otherness that hypostasizes this Principle, then why do we hang on to theology even on an academic level? Why shouldn't we be satisfied with anthropology, or biology, or physics?

My dear Norman, "the principal theological challenges of the twenty-first century" are and will remain those of every century: the existential questions of humanity, the problem of the cause and the goal of existence and of that which exists. Does empirical pragmatism give us answers to these questions? Does the Church's assurance that death "is trampled on by death" possess the flesh of reality, or does it not? Twaddle such as that of Helminiak is of no relevance to serious people.

Ecumenical Dialogue

NR: *Georges Florovsky once notoriously stated that Christian reunion meant conversion to Orthodoxy. How would you want to see ecumenism develop today?*

CY: I am pretty sure that Fr Florovsky understood the *reunification* of Christians as their turning toward the reality of the Church, to the effort of attaining the ecclesial *mode of existence.* He did not mean their joining today's fragmented nationalistic "Orthodoxism" that passes for Orthodoxy.

Christ originally defined the Church as a field sown with wheat where inevitably, right up to the last judgment, tares will also spring up among the wheat. Heresies, distortions, alienation, and exploitation of the ecclesial event can never be definitively eradicated—can "dialogues" and political "agreements" and "good relations" ever banish prostitution from societies and allow only the attainment of loving self-denial to flourish?

"Ecumenical dialogue" could also be a manifestation of the ecclesial event if it sprang from the need all of us have for self-criticism, for the recognition of historical mistakes, sinful actions, misinterpretations, and misunderstandings, with a view to recognizing more fully the experience of the ecclesial *mode of existence*. If the motive were the need for repentance of this kind, we would not entrust "dialogue" to professional careerists serving institutions of power (bishops, university professors, "cadres" of synodical offices, etc.). We would look for persons for whom the unity of Christians is a painful existential problem, a problem of how to access the light of the Church's truth, that is to say, a problem concerned with our "salvation." We would look for ascetical monks, presbyters sanctified by their self-denial, and charismatic theologians.

Orthodoxy and Human Rights

NR: *I should like to turn to the subject of human rights. Many people might assume that human rights are indisputably a good thing and hardly the subject of controversy. Yet you have demonstrated very powerfully in your* Inhuman Character of Rights *that the notion of human rights—one of the foundation stones of modernity—"presupposes a reductionist view of the human subject as fundamentally an undifferentiated natural individual,"[2] with results that are ultimately inimical to human values, and indeed productive of inhumanity. The Russians have been particularly exercised by this problem, largely, I suppose, because*

---

[2]Christos Yannaras, *Hē apanthrōpia tou dikaiōmatos* (Athens: Domos, 2006), 7.

the Russian people are painfully aware of their denial of human rights during the Soviet era. Patriarch Kirill has warned, however, that the understanding and application of human rights is not without ideological implications, bearing, as it does, "the serious cultural imprint of the West."[3] *On the pastoral level, the Russian Bishops' Council has issued a protest against "secularised standards of human rights," warning that while "there is a widespread conviction that the human rights institution in itself can promote in the best possible way the development of human personality and social organisation . . . human rights protection is often used as a plea to realise ideas which in essence radically disagree with Christian teaching . . . obstructing the most important goal in human life, which is deliverance from sin and finding salvation."*[4] *This seems at first sight to echo your own views. Do you support the Russian bishops' declaration?*

CY: I am glad you have posed this question. It gives me an opportunity to show again that criticism of Western culture (self-criticism for all of us today) can be fruitful not if it is constructed according to Western logic (that is, using Western criteria of qualitative evaluation), but only if it is constructed according to the logic and criteria of nonsubmission to the Western paradigm.

Does the protection of the rights of the individual represent something "good" or something "evil"? The question is hopelessly enmeshed in Western logic. For "good" and "evil" in this logic are measured by the "objective" standards (of supernatural *auctoritas* or common rationalist conventions), standards or "constants" that determine utilitarian benefit. For some these are standards of this-worldly utilitarian benefit; for others they refer to "eternal" utilitarian benefit—depending on how they arrange

[3]Patriarch Kirill of Moscow, *Freedom and Responsibility: A Search for Harmony, Human Rights and Personal Dignity* (London: Darton, Longman & Todd, 2011), 87.
[4]Ibid., 115.

their hierarchy of "values" (which is another concept, similarly bereft of real content, that objectifies the "good").

In the ecclesial paradigm (which the West has wrongly called "Byzantium"), the words "good" and "evil" (today we would also add the word "values") refer only to coincidental intentionalities. "What is called wholly good," says Maximus the Confessor, "is not absolutely good, but is sometimes good and sometimes evil. And what is called wholly evil is not absolutely evil, but is sometimes evil and sometimes good." By the criterion, then, of the Church's culture, the safeguarding of individual rights in modernity was for that specific period (the eighteenth and nineteenth centuries) something that was very good both in the West and in the East, for the West emerged finally from the darkness of the Middle Ages (from the post-Roman West, the "barbarian West," as J. M. Wallace-Hadrill calls it), where rights were enjoyed only by the few (the nobility and the clergy). The Greco-Roman world emerged in the same period from the centuries-long yoke of servitude to the Turks. As for the Slavic peoples, they still lived for the most part in dire conditions of serfdom.

But with the same criteria, the criteria of the Church's culture, what was great and good for all in the eighteenth and nineteenth centuries, the achievement of the protection of individual rights, was infantile and unimportant in comparison with the status and privileges bestowed on the ancient Greek "citizen" by his participation in the "common struggle" to realize the "city" and "politics." The West never understood the Greek version of politics as a "struggle to attain truth," nor did it become aware of the historical continuity of this struggle in the "parish" or "community" of the Greco-Roman world or *oikoumenē*, even to some extent during the centuries of the *Tourkokratia*.

By the criteria, then, of the Greco-Roman world and the Church's culture, the modern protection of *individual rights* was on the one hand an achievement for its time, but on the other

merely a prepolitical achievement for communities that still aspire
to the priority of "utility" and are unaware of the organization
of a collectivity with the goal of realizing the "true"—the *mode*
"of the arrangement of the universe" (Heraclitus), or the *mode*
of the triadic Godhead, the mode of love. By the criteria of the
Greek and ecclesial paradigm, the securing of individual rights is
something "good" for communities with very low ("barbarian")
utilitarian demands, and is also something "evil," an inadequate
system of organizing collectivity for "political" communities.

It is only by abandoning the rationale of the Western paradigm that we can judge those of its products that have obviously entered into our lives today. The patriarch of Russia and
the Russian synod of bishops, in the expressions that you mention
to me, show that they have an intuition through their sense of
the Church that something is wrong with the absolute priority
that the rights of the individual have in the West. They speak of
"secularized standards of human rights," that is, they attribute an
ideological character (as a moral evaluation) to the type of individual rights that the West maintains—as if a distinction exists
between individual rights that are "secularized" and those that
are "nonsecularized." They identify in the protection of human
rights the realization "of ideas which in essence radically disagree
with Christian teaching," which means that the leadership of the
Russian Church is able to understand the differences from the
West only on an ideological level (the level of "ideas")—once
again in abstract and general terms.

It is not at all by chance that the Russian Church today, after
seventy years of persecution and martyrdom, is interested above
all in recovering the worldly power it had enjoyed under the
Tsars, by imitating the Vatican to the fullest possible extent. That
is why the theological renaissance that the refugees of the Russian
diaspora brought to Europe is provocatively ignored, or is even
slandered, by today's "official" administration of the Russian

Church. The intoxication of worldly power is not compatible with the evangelical witness of the Church's experience which once renewed the Russian diaspora.

Ecological Issues

NR: *An area in which Orthodox teaching seems to be having an impact—perhaps because it ties in with secular concerns—is in environmental issues, with Patriarch Bartholomew even establishing a reputation as "the Green Patriarch." So far as I am aware, you have not written much on these matters. Is that because you think others are sufficiently engaged with them?*

CY: No, I have in fact often written on them, but in various essays, not in a systematic study. What I have tried to say until now is that the logic that provoked our appalling ecological problem cannot be the same logic that generates its solution. This is what the environmental movements unfortunately do: they want to preserve the utilitarian logic of "development," simply changing its evaluation of what is more useful from an egocentric, human point of view, so that it is no longer a mindless "exploitation," but a well-reasoned (by rationalist and self-interested principles) "protection." It is the same logic as that which was taught in the catechetical schools in my youth: Don't go to brothels to avoid catching syphilis!

Personally, I believe that the destruction of the ecosystem cannot be slowed down or halted unless there is a change of attitude in us toward nature. I like to use the example of a painting. For a person governed by egocentric instincts, this is simply a wooden frame and a colored piece of canvas. If this person is cold, he or she would burn it to keep warm. For a person of *relation*, the erotic or loving person, the painting on the canvas is the *logos*, or principle, of a personal uniqueness. It preserves the otherness of a specific person: of Goya, of Rembrandt, of van Gogh. Only when a person discovers in the painting the immediacy and clarity of the *logos* of a personal otherness, only then will his or her attitude change toward the painting, and only then will he or she respect it and protect it. That is to say, only when people discover in the beauty of nature the *Logos* of the otherness of the personal God, the creator of the cosmos, will there cease to be an ecological problem.

The Ecumenical Patriarchate appears today to be colluding with the utilitarian naivities of the environmentalists. But we should not forget that the Ecumenical Patriarchate continues to live in a Muslim state under the constant threat of its historical extinction. For centuries now it has won a reprieve for its survival by constantly finding some respectable means of maintaining a presence on the international scene, so that the Turks do not dare touch it.

The means of defense that it finds suitable may sometimes have a secular rather than ecclesiastical character. But it must be admitted that none of these has ever led to any compromise with regard to ecclesial tradition and witness.

NR: *I take your point that the Ecumenical Patriarchate has entered into the environmental debate partly because it is inhibited by the Turkish government from concerning itself with more overtly political issues. Others too have noted that the patriarch tends to rely on anthropocentric (though not egocentric) language, largely, perhaps, because he is addressing secular audiences. But he fully supports theological reflection on the environment, such as that of the eucharistic view of the cosmos associated with the names of Alexander Schmemann and John Zizioulas. An approach that has attracted attention recently is that of "panentheism," first used by Schelling and taken up at the beginning of the twentieth century by the Russian School. Elizabeth Theokritoff has written, " 'Panentheism' is not a traditional term. But it captures well the cosmological vision of Maximus and Palamas, as well as the*

sacramental cosmology explored by Schmemann and others."[5]
Do you find anything helpful in "panentheism"?

CY: Let me correct you on one point: I did not say that the patriarchate is working for the protection of the environment because it wants to involve itself in matters chiefly political and is only prevented from doing so by the Turkish government. I do not think that the patriarchate's activity in environmental matters is a substitute for some wished-for political action. I am simply suggesting that it is a way for the patriarchate to project itself and gain esteem internationally, and is consequently a form of defense against the policy of the Turkish state, which desires through a process of attrition to extinguish the historic presence of the patriarchate.

To be sure, there is a solid theological backbone to the environmental activity of Patriarch Bartholomew: the eucharistic cosmology of John Zizioulas (even if in a summary and restricted form). Yet the general public and people in authority today (in politics and "information technology") understand nothing of this essentially ecclesial perspective. They respect and admire the patriarch's involvement, but with the utilitarian criteria of the Green movements. Nevertheless, "either by pretext or in truth" (Phil 1.18), the patriarchate defends itself against Turkish pressure.

Let me also say that the modern proposal of "panentheism" has no relationship with the cosmological perspective of Maximus and Gregory Palamas. Panentheism ("everything is in God") believes that God flows into and penetrates even the most minute detail of the cosmic whole (without God being identified with the process of cosmic becoming itself as in classic pantheism). It is a "mystical" version that perhaps draws on Buddhist ideas and

---

[5]Elizabeth Theokritoff, *Living in God's Creation: Orthodox Perspectives on Ecology* (Crestwood, NY: St Vladimir's Seminary Press, 2005), 245.

that, as always in mysticism, does not aspire to any coherent and rational (that is, empirically communicable) ontology.

I have come to understand, my dear Norman, that what guarantees the realism of the Church's witness is coherence in its ontological logic and language—I would venture to say that all the heresies in the history of the Church have enormous gaps in their ontological sequentiality. This does not mean that methodological ontological sequentiality is sufficient to ensure the correctness of Christian teaching. I believe, however, that the converse is true: the witness of the Church's experience always contains the realism of ontological sequentiality in its formulation.

A vital issue that merits serious discussion was posed years ago by the Serbian bishop Athanasios Jevtić. He observed that historical habits of thought over the centuries have shaped the mentality (the *noo-tropia*, or mode of thinking) of the Greeks: the latter operate with the coordinates of a particular ontological approach. A difficulty in aligning themselves with this mode of thinking characterized both the Germanic tribes of the early post-Roman period in the West and the Slavic tribes in the period of their Christianization. And this difficulty in dealing with the ontological issue has endured for centuries in the Christianized West and among the Christianized Slavs. Moreover, the Westernization of the Greeks leads increasingly in their own technology, too, to an ever-more-obvious distancing from the problematic and language of ontology.

I should mention the name of Vladimir Lossky as an exception.

NR: *In what way is he an exception? Would you see yourself as an heir to Lossky's approach?*

CY: That is for others to judge, not me. But I do not think the word "heir" in this context is appropriate. We are all influenced and helped by other people. I do not know what stimulated Lossky, or even if it is easily discernible in his work. At any rate, he received the grace, after many centuries of the alienation of the Church's witness (the witness of the truth of the Church as it is lived), to be the first to write no longer an ideological "dogmatics," an exposition/confession of "convictions," but a book where the experience of the ecclesial body is set down (signified/delineated).

My own motive was to reply to Heidegger's challenge. It was a challenge that concerned our existential problem: Heidegger's existential nihilism summarized a directly experienced empirical reality that was definitive of the life of modern humanity. It was not a challenge for abstract academic discussion, but a command to express solidarity with, and respond to, the anxiety about the impasse, the absurd, and the void that torments modern humanity. I believe that I had to investigate and find out whether the tradition of ecclesial experiential witness had a reply to Heidegger's nihilism.

The Ecumenical Patriarchate

NR: *On the subject of the Ecumenical Patriarchate, you have declared yourself in favor of abolishing the autocephaly of the Church of Greece and moving the seat of the Ecumenical Patriarchate to Thessalonica—not because you see the patriarchate as bound up with a nationalistic version of Hellenism, but because you are convinced that this will renew its real ecumenical role (Kyriaki, June 20, 1999). Do you still hold that opinion?*

CY: I would venture to say that this is not simply an "opinion." The Church does not recognize the category of a "free thinker," or *penseur libre*, an intellectual who is not bound by any presuppositions. However, the Church does recognize "philosophical people" (lovers, not possessors, of wisdom), who bear witness, in the form both of assertions and proposals, with trust in the undetermined reality of the body of the Church (the hidden leaven, the buried seed, the lost coin), which at times will judge their witness as "gold, silver, and precious stones," or as "sticks, straw, and reeds."

The problem is not whether the Ecumenical Patriarchate should move from today's Istanbul to a country with an active ecclesial (Orthodox) population. The problem is: What ecclesiastical institution can preserve and express *today* the unity of "the Catholic Church throughout the *oikoumenē*"? How can we preserve the truth of ecclesial catholicity, so that we keep it as a *mode* of existence, a *mode* or manifestation of salvation?

This *mode* has been bequeathed to us, and it is *synodical:* the synod of those who preside at the Eucharist. The central support, the backbone, of the synodical *mode* (the axis of the ordering of "primacies," that is, of responsibilities) was the institution of the so-called *pentarchy of patriarchates*. With the lapse of Old Rome into barbarian "religionization," the synodical axis of catholic cohesion was left with four patriarchates. Moscow destroyed this axis and dissolved ecclesial cohesion in 1589: it demanded, or rather, compelled its "elevation" to a patriarchate, introducing (and imposing from that time) the idea of the patriarchate as the highest rank of authority (by criteria that were absolutely secular) within the Church. This was an event with consequences as great for the truth of the Church in the consciousness of people and for the Church's cultural and historical development as, I believe, the *schism* of 1054.

In the nineteenth century the concept of a "patriarchate" was linked undisguisedly with the "autocephaly" of every ethnic collectivity that bore the name of Christian. For the Romanians a patriarchate, for the Serbs a patriarchate, and likewise for the Bulgarians and the Georgians. The Orthodox Catholic Church was fragmented into as many pieces as there are nationalities among its believers. This fragmentation has been replicated in the "diaspora"—there are as many bishops in the big urban centers as there are national "patriarchates" in Orthodoxism.

The problem of the Church's catholicity, of the unity of the local churches throughout the *oikoumenē*, remains insoluble and plunges people into confusion and various errors. The synodical system, based on the pentarchy of patriarchs, functioned adequately in the first eight centuries and produced the seven ecumenical councils, but within the historicopolitical context of the Roman Empire centered on New Rome, or Constantinople. When the empire was dissolved in the West, there was born in Old Rome, as a result of specific historical needs, the proposition of an ideological "catholicity" founded on the controlling role of an "infallible cathedra" and an administrative mechanism with the marks, for the first time in history, of *totalitarianism*.

When New Rome, after conquest by the Turks, moved over to the margins of history, the Vatican model of "unity" remained the only model, enjoying for a time an unchallenged ascendency. It was rejected by the Protestant reformers, who still adhered to the ideological sense of unity but rejected a centralized totalitarianism. They therefore slid unavoidably toward fragmentation. The unity of every Protestant "confession" is primarily ideological and secondarily organizational, without the absence of symptoms of an appalling totalitarianism in the organization of some of the sects. The model of the Vatican was imported into each "confession," with the loss, however, of the quantitative and geographical dimension of catholicity (catholic in the sense of global), which remained the "prerogative" of Old Rome alone.

There has been an analogous reception of the Vatican model by the "Orthodox" as well. Each bishop functions as a pope, "sovereign and despot," chiefly as bearer of administrative authority, with an interest in ideological cohesion reduced to a minimum; the ideology of a religionized church becomes simply an infantile moralism. The role of papal "infallibility" is *also* claimed from the bishops by certain zealot monks held in the world to be "elders."

The unity of the Church is the vital problem facing us today.

Primacy and Collegiality

NR: *Yes, the fragmentation of modern national Orthodox churches—or Orthodoxisms—is lamentable. And the jurisdictional disputes of recent years, particularly in Eastern Europe but also, as you say, in the West, are a real scandal. What, however, is the solution? Does not episcopal collegiality need some kind of primacy in order to function?*

Which leads me to ask, is there not a role for the Petrine office? Nicolas Afanassieff, in a famous essay, set out his vision of "the Church which presides in love."[6] Before becoming Pope Benedict XVI, Cardinal Ratzinger spoke of the papacy of the first Christian millennium as offering a model for relations with Orthodoxy. What would Rome have to do to reenter the pentarchy of patriarchates?

CY: These are vital questions. I repeat that it is only my personal thoughts I am setting down here, without any assurance that they are right.

Certainly, there can be no hope of achieving the unity of the Church throughout the *oikoumenē* if the synodical system is not working properly. And the synodical system cannot function unless two distinct problems are resolved: First, who presides over the synod? Second, why should the bishop of one particular church preside rather than another? That is to say, what is the significance and role of the order of precedence of episcopal sees within the Church?

---

[6]Nicolas Afanassieff, "The Church which presides in Love," in *The Primacy of Peter in the Orthodox Church*, ed. J. Meyendorff et al. (London: The Faith Press, 1963), 57–110.

We need a serious study of how the synodical system worked and what the order of precedence was in the centuries before the schism. We need such a study not so as to impose the old order as of value in itself, but so as to discern the *criteria*, the ecclesial rationale, both of the institution of the synods and of the ordering of precedence.

I would venture to say that a church's title of antiquity or the fact that it was founded by one of Christ's apostles (as Rome was by Peter or New Rome by Andrew) has absolutely no ecclesial *meaning* or character (i.e., no *meaning* or character that reveals truth, or that is evangelical, in the sense that it proclaims the gospel). They are criteria of an entirely secular mentality, and a very juvenile one at that. For someone to claim a title of validity, authenticity, and power on the strength of the authority of his first predecessor is so absurd as to be quite comical. The authority of the apostolic founders of the churches of Asia Minor, or the mention of these churches in the Revelation of John, did not prevent their historical extinction.

The Roman Catholic Church adopted, or rather invented, as a criterion of unity of the (local) churches on earth, ideological homogeneity—a homogeneity that could be controlled by an "infallible" cathedra. This version of geographical-quantitative universality led to the following well-known consequences:

It distorted the struggle of faith/trust (a struggle to transcend the ego and attain participation in the body of the Church—a struggle to belong) into an individualistic attainment—the possession of "correct" convictions. Intellectualism supplanted the empiricism of ecclesial witness.

For the first time in human history, it gave birth to totalitarianism: relentless administrative mechanisms for the control of people's thinking, a policing of the spoken and written word, and the persecution (with torture and death) of dissidents.

It alienated the ecclesial event, into an individualistic religion. The aim of this religion was the salvation of the individual, and the means for attaining it were an individualistic morality, an individualistic doctrinal orthodoxy, and individualistic forms of worship. The religionization of the Church is the key institutional alienation, more significant than any other corruption that Christian experience and witness has suffered through the centuries.

A synod, then, is an assembly of bishops in which each of them serves the truth and unity of a local church as a body, that is to say, as an image of the *mode* of existence of the thearchic Triad. The bishop is a *father* of the body, that is to say, a servant of all, a guide for every member on the path of changing his or her mode of existence. He is not an ideological commissar, nor an administrator, nor a despot (the popular Greek word for a bishop), nor a lord and master, nor a propagandist for ideological doctrines. He is first because he is last, the servant of all in the ecclesial assembly. And he participates in the synod not in order to express personal opinions, views, or clever ideas, but to express the experience of his local church. He participates in order to judge any topic by the criterion of this experience.

That is why a synod too is an extension of the Eucharist: somebody presides at the Eucharist, and all concelebrate the realization and manifestation of the Church as a *mode* of true existence. A synod has the same aim in view, and it seeks it by the same means: not in ideological unison, but in the manifestation of ecclesial truth as a mode of existential unity, an image of the triadic end of the fullness of existence. For the presidency, the office of primacy, to be ecclesial, the manifestation in practice of the words of Christ is required: the first is the last of all, the servant of all. The remark made by Cardinal Ratzinger sounds sadly illusory, like the loss of contact with reality, or else is a decorative embellishment for propagandist purposes. For the Church of Rome to be again the church that "presides in love," as Ignatius of Antioch calls it, it must transform its existence from an individual-centered religion, a "tare" in God's field, into *Ekklēsia*—a different order of reality. Such a transformation can only be experienced as an eschatological hope.

An analogous case is presented by the patriarchates of Orthodoxism. Orthodoxism opposes Roman Catholicism ideologically, but in reality the Vaticanization of its institutions and functions is a fact: the same religionization of the ecclesial event, the same individualistic version of salvation, the same sharp games of authority in the field of ideological projection.

Assuredly, the Church that sustains our hope is a hidden Church. It is like the seed lying in the ground, or like the living yeast within the dead flour.

NR: *Your fundamental insight that the Church is a relationship of love, not a set of ideas, is of great importance. But how does this work out in practice? If the Church is the same as the kingdom of God, is it not an eschatological reality only?*

CY: But relationship *is* practice—the word "practice" comes from the verb *prattō*, which means "I act, I do." Every relationship is practice, is an act with a purpose and a result. The Church is a communion of relations of love; it is the reality of existence as an act of love, sustenance (the taking of food and drink) as communion, conduct as relations of serving others. In the Church we do not partake of ideas, convictions, or doctrines, or even commandments and obligations; we partake of the necessities of life, the requirements of existence, and we share in them because we love and trust, because we find joy in actively realizing life as love and trust.

What does *fasting* mean for the Church? It means my freedom in practical terms, that is, my actively choosing to eat only what the Church as a whole is eating on particular days. Consequently, the taking of food is for me not an individual act of self-preservation, but an event of communion, participation in the *mode*, by which the Church (in the Eucharist) partakes of food. The same happens when we pray, when we express our communion and solidarity with the needs of our child, our spouse, or of any of our fellow human beings.

In the degree in which the actions/relations of our life are loving, that is to say, ecclesial, they are an image and manifestation of the triadic *mode* of existence, that is, of the Church as it will be manifested in its completion in the last days as God's "kingdom," that is, as the sovereignty of the *mode* of divinity over created and uncreated.

NR: *Can you give me some examples of bishops who have met the criteria you set out?*

CY: The criteria set by the Church, if I have understood them correctly, are not requirements or presuppositions that are either met or not met. They are rather goals that, through being worked toward (this is what freedom is in practice) and through many failures, are attained without the achievement ever being exhausted. "This is the perfect, endless perfection of the perfect."[7] Even the most holy of the bishops remains a human being with the limitations of createdness. The concept of "infallibility" is incompatible with the truth of the Church; it is a product of humanity's instinctive religious need to worship idols.

As a rule, what prevails today is the alienation of the episcopal function. Instead of being primarily a function of fatherhood, it is an administrative office. Contact between the bishop and the lay body of whose head he is appears to be minimal, or even nonexistent. The bishop is the administrative superior of the presbyters, the "archpriest" of the "priests," as the language of religion would have it, nullifying the terminology that is the properly ecclesial. He retains an authoritarian jurisdiction unaffected by the rule of

[7]John Climacus, *Spiritual Ladder*, Step 29 (PG 88:1148C).

law and control of arbitrary behavior that modernity has succeeded in establishing.

As a result, neither do the "synods" of bishops have any relation with the ecclesial institution of the synod or council. The bishop in the synod no longer conveys the witness of the eucharistic body, whose assembly he serves as father and pastor. He brings to the synod his individual views and opinions, participating in it like a director of any business at a meeting of the board. Certain factors, I believe, play a vital role in this alienating secularization: the obligatory celibacy of the bishops is detached from the monastic struggle of divine love that guides and supports virginity; the imperial splendor of vestments is stripped of a liturgical character lived out in practice; the administration of wealth often, through the love of the faithful, is centralized in the hands of the bishop; and so forth.

Nevertheless, despite this established state of alienation, there are consoling exceptions of charismatic bishops. Personally, I would locate most of these hope-inspiring exceptions in the Church of Serbia.

NR: *In view of Western criticism of Greece's support for Serbia in the 1990s, could you expand on what you see as inspiring signs in the Serbian Church?*

CY: I am not able to give a more objective picture of the ecclesial authenticity that I have encountered subjectively in certain bishops of the Serbian Church today. Nor can I do so with regard to the conduct and ecclesial spirit of ordinary people in Greece who gave practical support to their fellow-Orthodox Serbian brothers and sisters in their time of trial.

Allow me simply to make a prediction. If the writing of unbiased scholarly history continues to exist in the future, it will one day show that the entirely arbitrary, inhuman, and horrific bombing of urban centers and infrastructures in Serbia by the NATO war machine (1999) was a crime against humanity incomparably more monstrous than Hitler's *Anschluss* with Austria or invasion of Czechoslovakia (1939). It had the same motives as those that governed the capture, sack, and irreparable destruction of New Rome/Constantinople by the soldiers of the Fourth Crusade (1204). I put my personal judgment on record to be verified or falsified.

NR: *Has there been any synod in the Church's history that has functioned along the lines you consider necessary? The seven ecumenical councils all seem to have been concerned either with excluding error or (in the case of the Fourth at Chalcedon) with accommodating and reconciling different approaches to the expression of the Church's experience of Christ.*

CY: You touch upon an extremely interesting topic, Norman, a topic that merits extensive study.

I would reply provisionally and in a superficial way that there has never been a synod in the history of the Church that has functioned along impeccably ecclesiological lines in keeping with what is intimated in the Gospels. And I would add: fortunately! Every synod is an image of the "kingdom," as described by Christ: a field sown with wheat but also with tares. A faultless perfection in the functioning of a synod could only be found outside anything human—an idolized ideological position, like the sanctity of all the popes or an inhuman puritanism. The assurance Christ gave to Paul, "My power is made perfect in weakness" (2 Cor 12.9), is revealing and therefore especially consoling. The marvelous thing, in my view, is that in spite of human weaknesses, and perhaps sinful intentions and ambitions, the priority of the need to distinguish truth from falsehood, to define the experience of the Church, to distance itself from its alienation, actually prevailed at the councils.

METAPHYSICS AS A PERSONAL ADVENTURE

I think that the most painful failure is not a sinful council, but, for fourteen centuries now, the absence of a council: the lack of interest in the functioning of a council and the clarification of ecclesial experience—indifference to the way the path of life is confused with the path of death.

Dostoevsky

NR: *We have discussed the influence of Heidegger on your thinking, but has not Dostoevsky been even more important? I have in mind* The Brothers Karamazov, *particularly the early discussion on the relation between Church and state and later Ivan's fable of the Grand Inquisitor. Your discussions of the nature of freedom, of evil and suffering, and of the "religionization" of the Church all seem to draw on profoundly Dostoevskian themes. Is Dostoevsky the theologian for our times?*

CY: The Greek Nobel-prize-winning poet, George Seferis, wrote the following wise lines:

> Our words are the children of many people.
> They are sown and they are born like infants;
> They take root and are nourished by blood.[8]

Who can say what influences from what people are reflected in his words? Nietzsche opened our eyes for us to see that in reality "God is dead," that in the post-Roman West he was killed by intellectualism, by the need for the individual to be armor-plated with "objective" certainties about his existence, for the God of ecclesial experience and witness to be replaced by intellectual idols of God, the rational "proofs" for his existence. For me personally, the most realistic confirmation of Nietzsche's proclamation

---

[8]From George Seferis' last volume of poetry, *Three Secret Poems*, published in 1966.

is M.-D. Chenu's brief but gripping study *La théologie comme science au XIIIe siècle* (Paris: Editions Vrin, 1969).

It is only by going through Nietzsche's books; M.-D. Chenu's studies; and Heidegger's book on Nietzsche (Pfullingen: Neske-Verlag, 1961),[9] especially the chapter that analyzes the first part of Nietzsche's *Der Wille zur Macht* and bears the title "European nihilism" ("Der europaische Nihilismus")—it is only by this or a similar route that one can appreciate the astonishing discernment of Dostoevsky's critique of the papal church. In one of his letters written from Dresden in 1870, he wrote, "All of Europe's misfortunes, all without exception, derive from the fact that the Church of Rome lost Christ and subsequently thought that it could go on without him."

Would you like us to discuss what this statement of Dostoevsky's may mean?

NR: *In a recent book on Dostoevsky, Rowan Williams points out that from the point of view of the management of human affairs, the covert despotism of the Inquisitor guarantees the prosaic happiness of the ordinary and the weak, the impossible demands of the gospel only making sense to a tiny minority of spiritual athletes.[10] Your ecclesiology (and implicitly that of Williams too) lays emphasis on a freedom that allows us to reorientate our whole nature, to change our mode of existence from the mode of the created to the mode of the uncreated. But where does that leave the ordinary and the weak? Is the Church as you envision it only for a tiny minority of spiritual athletes?*

CY: I believe that Dostoevsky is referring to the Church of Rome when even the last remnants of Latin Orthodoxy had finally disappeared from it—when Rome was henceforth in thrall to the

[9]English version: Martin Heidegger, *Nietzsche*, vols. 1 and 2, trans. David Farrell Krell (San Francisco: Harper & Row, 1991).

[10]Rowan Williams, *Dostoevsky: Language, Faith and Fiction* (London and New York: Continuum, 2008), 27.

"enlightened" Franks. Europe "lost Christ" not because it forgot him or denied him, but because the Christ of ecclesial experience had been alienated to become the "founder" of a religion. This alienation was indeed inevitable, was a historical necessity, and I shall explain why.

The Greco-Roman world had received the Church's gospel out of a conscious, real need. The gospel filled serious gaps in philosophical and religious metaphysics. It set exciting existential goals for humankind. But the barbarian nomadic tribes that brought about the collapse of the Roman Empire in the West from the fourth to the sixth centuries AD, populations at a very low level of cultural development, were "converted" to Christianity en masse and were baptized in large groups in the rivers, since for them becoming Christian brought them access to culture, to another "paradigm" of life, with the expectation of a better standard of living and development. Christianity was for them a new "religion," a "higher" substitute for their pagan beliefs, morals, and religious rites.

They fashioned from the ecclesial fact a typically "natural religion" that was individualistic, legalistic, moralistic, and emotional. In the astonishing historical studies of the great modern Western medievalists (Georges Duby, Jacques Le Goff, Robert Lopez, J. M. Wallace-Hadrill, Etienne Gilson, etc.), one may get a strong sense of the beginnings of this inexorable "religionization" of the ecclesial event in the "barbarian West"—a religionization of the Church of Rome, that is to say, what Dostoevsky calls the "loss of Christ." Because the Christ who is approached and known not through the experience of participation in his body, the eucharistic ecclesial community, but made autonomous as objective teaching, ethics, and dogma, with the Church simply as an administrative mechanism for defending this objectified truth—this Christ, says Dostoevsky bluntly, is the Antichrist, the perverted truth of the Church's Christ.

And this perversion continues even today. Let me give you an example. From what you yourself say, in agreement with me, as I gather from our discussions, the vast majority of Christians in Europe today, regardless of which "confession" they belong to (not excepting the "Orthodox") are absolutely sure that the *salvation* that the Church preaches is individual, that each of us will be saved or punished eternally in accordance with our individual virtues or our individual sins, with our many or our nonexistent merits. And what precisely is entailed by "salvation" appears to be very confused. It is usually taken to be an extension of individual existence, of the ego, in eternity, that is, in endless linear time. But even the intellectual conception alone of an existence that never ends generates panic in humankind; it is a nightmare—and especially when this endless existence is defined as a "blessed repose," a definitive pensioning off, a joy springing from inactivity.

How can people regard the promise of such terminal passivity as "good news," when on this earth they have tasted the joy of creation, the elation of research, the inebriation of the constant discovery of beauty, the ecstasy of love, the wonder of bringing children into the world?

Church and State

NR: *As I understand it, Dostoevsky regarded the Roman Catholic Church as a church turned into a state, and the contemporary Russian version of Orthodoxy as a state turned into a church—both of these versions of Christianity being concerned with the projection of power. This analysis still seems to me relevant to our thinking about the Church. On the one hand, we have the Roman Catholic Church, which even after the Second Vatican Council still seems to think of itself in terms of a* societas perfecta. *On the other, although many modern Orthodox like to speak about the symbiosis of Church and state, in practice the Orthodox Church in traditional Orthodox countries depends upon state support. What is the way forward for Orthodoxy? You have spoken in your books about the Church being the eucharistic community of a particular time and place, and in our discussions you have drawn attention to the importance of a properly functioning synodal system. But is not some overarching authority also needed? In the past the emperor acted as* epistēmonarchēs, *calling councils and overseeing the discipline of the Church. Without him, modern Orthodoxy seems somewhat dysfunctional. Who or what can fulfill his role today? Could you say more about Moscow? What is it that disturbs you about developments in Russia?*

CY: My personal view, which I cannot guarantee to be correct, is that the alienation of the Church cannot be attributed to the relationship between Church and state. There is, I believe, only one form of alienation of the Church, a single unique eventuality of alienation: its transformation into an individualistic religiosity, its religionization. Before becoming a state the Roman Catholic Church became an ideology, that is, a totality of individual convictions; an individual appropriation of infallible certainties; an individual armor-plating with objectively affirmed virtues, with a quantifiable degree of the individual's fidelity to ethical-legal ordinances. Rome ceased to be a church, in its official teaching, from the moment it alienated the gospel, turning it into a prescription for the assurance of individual salvation. Something similar is happening with Moscow today.

I venture to suggest, perhaps mistakenly, that if an ecumenical synod ever takes place (the first after the schism of 1054 and the Reformation of 1517) with a view to shedding light on the question of which *is* the Church and where the Church *is not*, it would suffice for it to concern itself with one question and one alone: *Is salvation an individual attainment, or is it an ecclesial event?* Do we arrive at salvation thanks to our individual merits, reinforced by the help that God grants to us individually; or is salvation our participation in the body of the Church, in the *mode* of love of the triadic Cause of that which exists? Are we saved by our individual worth or by the love of Christ, the Theotokos, and the saints, which embraces us and brings us into existential fullness, into freedom from death?

In this second perspective, the ecclesial one, the emperor or the state can serve the communitarian event, without substituting themselves for it or exploiting it for the benefit of individualistic purposes. In the first perspective, however, the individual-centered one, religiosity is easily transformed into an ideological particularity that functions as "an adhesive binding the nation together," as a guarantor of the ethics that are indispensable for social cohesion. The Church can never compromise with Caesar. It can never use Caesar's authority to impose the gospel—if it does so, it ceases to be the Church. As a collective structure, it is subject to Caesar's laws, which assure a "calm and peaceful life" in its totality. It may also be served by Caesar, if Caesar respects it as an event of collectivity radically different (in its presuppositions and aims) from secular state structures.

These very simple truths have been misunderstood, altered, and distorted not since the period of the Christian empire of Greco-Roman times, but since the period in which the Church in the post-Roman barbarian West became thenceforth a natural religion.

NR: *Since the collapse of communism, a triumphalist approach seems to have reemerged in the Russian Orthodox Church. Does this disturb you?*

CY: The developments in Russia don't disturb me; they simply cause me anxiety and sorrow. I had believed, like others of my generation, that the period of martyrdom that this Church had experienced during the seventy years of communist totalitarianism, and the great privilege God had granted it, that the Russian diaspora, in that same period, should function as the catalyst of a wonderful renaissance of Orthodox ecclesial theology in the West and also in the other Orthodox churches—we had believed that as a result of these two facts, something had changed radically in the outlook and tactics of the Russian Church. For the historical past of Russian Christianity had all the marks that had led the Christianized Germanic tribes of the barbarian West eventually to break away from the body of the Catholic Church in the eleventh century (in 1054). What were these marks?

1. The conversion of the Russians (as the Franks) was imposed on the people by their leaders, with (as a rule) obligatory mass baptisms. It did not occur as a result of the personal choice of people. As a consequence of this, the ecclesial event was received from the very beginning, both in the Frankish West and in Russia, as a new "religion," perhaps a higher one in comparison with the pagan religions it had succeeded, but one chosen to serve the same drives, the same instinctive needs, that were the product of the religiosity *natural* to human beings. The religionization of the ecclesial event is an event that defines the conversion at the outset both of the post-Roman West and of Russia.

2. The second common mark is this: The conversion to Christianity of both the West and of Russia, again from the beginning, was closely linked to the imperial ambitions of their leaders— with the vision of the Holy Roman Empire of the German nation in the West, and with the vision of Moscow as the Third Rome in Russia. The link with drive for power had as a natural result the development of a climate that was clearly anti-Greek both in the West and in Russia, since Hellenism, not as a state or as a nation but as a civilization, formed the international "order of things" (*ordo rerum*) that was called "empire" (*imperium*).

3. The drive for power found expression in the claims to leadership of the Frankish popes (which were formulated characteristically in beliefs about the primacy of Peter, in the pseudo–

Donation of Constantine, in the pseudo-Isidorean Decretals, and which were recapitulated in the notorious *Dictatus* of Gregory VII [1075]). The Russians' drive for power became apparent immediately after the fall of Constantinople and the way in which they forced the recognition of Moscow as a patriarchate by holding the Ecumenical Patriarch Jeremias II Tranos hostage until they won the concession they wanted (1589). The high-handedness of the Russians literally destroyed the rationale of Orthodox ecclesiology by linking the concept of a "patriarchate" with nationalist ambitions for autonomy and secular "power," and by becoming the matrix and first fruits of a radical Protestantization of ecclesiology. With the dominance of nationalism in the nineteenth century, every nation-state with a majority Orthodox population was promoted to be a patriarchate, thus cheapening the institution and exposing it to ridicule. In the Church there has not been an institution or practice that has not functioned as a realization and manifestation of the new *mode of existence* proclaimed by the Church. With the nationalist character lent to it by the Russians, the institution of the patriarchate was alienated into an "Orthodox" version of the Protestant idea of a "state religion" (*Staatsreligion*), the supreme assertion of the religionization of the ecclesial event.

4. Just like the Franks, once the Russians had slipped into the religionization of the ecclesial event, they hastened to affirm (chiefly by external/objective tokens that even the simplest people could understand and appropriate) their differentiation from the Greek tradition and practice of ecclesial life. The Franks introduced the novelty of making the sign of the cross with five fingers and from left to right, the novelty of communicating only from the bread of the Eucharist (and unleavened bread at that, "dematerialized" into a host) and denying wine to the laity, and the novelty of clean-shaven clergy and obligatory celibacy. They changed the liturgical vestments; substituted religious paintings

and statues for the Church's icons; adopted the use of the organ in church services; radically changed the styles of architecture, music, and liturgical ceremonial; and so on, and so forth.

A corresponding attempt to differentiate themselves is obvious among the Russians also with a strong element of religionization, that is to say, with priority given to psychological/emotional and pietistic/moralistic aspects. They provocatively religionized worship with very long, drawn-out services loaded with emotional content, and with monotonous signings of the cross and genuflexions—worship as communion was unknown, so was "compunction" as freedom from atomistic piety, from aiming at "the salvation of the individual."

The Russians insisted on a differentiation of external elements that was clear and easily discernible by all: a Russian cross, a Russian chasuble, a Russian mitre, Russian (in their variety of colors) *kalymmafkia*, Russian icon screens, Russian religious paintings (clad in silver and gold "shirts") instead of icons, Russian domes, and so on, and so forth. The smallest details of the ways then in use of expressing (witnessing to) ecclesial experience were regarded by the Russians as a residue of Greekness, and therefore every effort was made, methodically and obstinately, to replace them with specifically Russian elements.

The construction of churches, especially at St Petersburg—all of them products of the period of the secular power of the clergy, thanks to the favor of the tsars—reflect the journey of a Russian Christianity that followed the footsteps of the corresponding Christianity of the Franks and led inexorably to a second schism like that of 1054—to the cutting off of the Russians too from the body of the catholic Church. (Fr Georges Florovsky, the most consistent theologian, I think, of the Russian diaspora in rejecting nationalism in his book *Ways of Russian Theology*,[11]

[11]Georges Florovsky, *Ways of Russian Theology*, trans. Robert L. Nichols, vols. 5 and 6 of the Collected Works of Georges Florovsky (Belmont, MA: Nordland, 1979).

describes this journey of Russian Christianity toward Western-ization, alienation, and estrangement with regard to the patristic Greek tradition.)

This journey was checked by Lenin, with the Bolshevik seizure of power in 1917. Of course, parallel to the persecution and the martyrdom, a number of bishops of the Russian Church, as soon as the opportunity presented itself, hastened to collaborate with the Soviet regime, and even with the KGB, to secure their privileges and power. And this apparently innate tendency of the Russian episcopate toward the acquisition of secular power acquired the dimensions of an avalanche immediately after the fall of communism. Today the wordliness of the Patriarchate of Moscow gives rise to fear and causes anxiety for the future, since it appears in its ambitions for pan-Orthodox domination to exceed even the symptoms it manifested in the days of the tsars. It has practically condemned, or at least adroitly marginalized, the theology of the Russian diaspora and has returned to the intellectual ideologizing of theological teaching, to pagan expressions of the religionization of lay piety.

NR: *In* Karamazov *the dilemma is between a church turned into a state (Rome) or a state that has been sacralized (Russia under the tsars). What are the alternatives in our secularized world today?*

CY: If my thinking is along the right lines, the way out of the dilemma is this: a state church or a sacralized state cannot be an "intelligent" alternative solution that an individual intellect can produce. If we need a solution, the only one available to us is to press for the holding of a council. And for a council to be held, a necessary presupposition is the existence of bishops, a sense of episcopal fatherhood of a specific (local) ecclesial body, to whose experience the bishop witnesses and testifies. Today our Vaticanized churches (churches that have been made to conform to the model of state organizational "effectiveness") function not with councils or synods, but with *synodal committees:* executive bodies of "specialists" (i.e., of university professors or clerics with university teaching posts) who seek "solutions" for ecclesial problems with the mentality of technocrats or mandarins. We seem to have lost the sense that bishop is the father of the eucharistic body who gives expression to its experience, not an administrator and ideological leader. We also seem to have lost the sense that a council is radically different from a general assembly of the higher executives of an organization.

NR: *Your discussion of Alyosha Karamazov in* The Meaning of Reality *(pp. 3–5) makes a very interesting contrast between what usually passes for spirituality ("a mirror in which we admire ourselves") and true spirituality ("the essential regeneration of man by the Spirit of God . . . inaccessible to human criteria and documentary verification"). You attack a "smug moralistic self-sufficiency" and commend Alyosha's declaration of his weakness and sinfulness—of his depravity. Yet in* The Enigma of Evil, *you protest against the constant harping on individual sin in the Church's liturgical prayers. How is regeneration by the Spirit to be encountered without the confession of our inadequacy and corruption as individuals?*

CY: I would say that the criterion for distinguishing ecclesial spirituality from any moralistic or other approximation to it is freedom from aims centered on the individual. A "spiritual" person for the Church is someone who to the greatest possible extent is free from the ego, that is, from the necessities that are entailed by the created and differentiate it existentially from the uncreated. The ecclesial person practices an ascetic life (and within the practice of self-transcendence is also the redemption of his or her failures) not in order to win merit as an individual, but to attain freedom from every kind of armoring of the ego with virtues or raptures or sense of psychological euphoria. The "discernment" (the ability to distinguish) between what is atomic, egoistic satisfaction and what is the joy of communion of existence and self-offering is described in patristic literature as "the greatest of the virtues."

The *Filioque*

NR: *You criticize the* Filioque, *with its emphasis on "internal relations" within the divine essence, as leaning toward a Judaic kind of monotheism. And you characterize the Son and the Spirit in profoundly Cappadocian terms, the Son existing as freedom of loving self-transcendence and self-offering, and the Spirit existing as active revelation of the hypostatic otherness of the Father. How does the Spirit differ from the Son? And how is the role of the Spirit manifested in the life of the Church?*

CY: "The limits of language are the limits of our world" (Wittgenstein), the limits of *created* reality.[12] The only thing we can say about the *uncreated* in the language of the *created* is to present some iconological or analogical comparisons drawn from the created, in the knowledge that the comparisons, even if they do not entirely fail, cannot possibly correspond to the reality of the uncreated.

We say that God *exists*. But in our language the verb "to exist" signifies that which we know to exist: an inexorably given existence, not the free choice to exist, or self-existence. We are speaking of three *hypostases* of the Godhead. But in our language the word "*hypostasis*" signifies the specific reality of existence as atomic onticity. To be sure, we are also aware of the human *personal* hypostasis as a dynamically activated *otherness*, and we understand this otherness always in a comparative sense (as in-relation-to). We cannot, however, conceive of it as it is in itself

---

[12]Cf. Ludwig Wittgenstein, Proposition 5.62, in *Tractatus Logico-Positivus*, trans. D. F. Pears and B. F. McGuiness (London and New York: Routledge, 2001).

as an event of relation (sonship) without the character of atomic individual onticity.

The addition of the *Filioque* (by the Council of Toledo, 589) betrays an exceedingly low level of understanding of the ecclesial witness to the triadic God—a level understandable for the then-barbaric Germanic tribes who formed this council. The same level of understanding was imposed by them on Western Christendom as a whole when they excluded Latin Orthodoxy from the episcopal throne of the Elder Rome. The then barbarians were not concerned about the existential problem. They did not join the Church because they had metaphysical questions about the "meaning" of their existence. It was religious concerns that drove them: they wanted to make sure that a divinity of equal magnitude, power, and authority was also attributed to the Son. They did not understand that the theological "Triad" signifies freedom of loving self-existence, that if the *mode* of the uncreated is loving communion as an existential event, as a trihypostatic (of free personal hypostases) unity (and fullness) of *being*, then it *may* also be granted to the created human persons to exist because they will to exist, and to will because they love. The insistence on the *monarchy* of the Father is the Church's gospel, or good news: the monarchy (*mon-archia*) of the Father means that his only principle (his *monē archē*) is the freedom of a personal will. It means that he wills to exist because he loves—the freedom of love is the causal mode of existence. Love *hypostasizes* (makes existence actually subsist as hypostases), "begetting" the Son and causing the Spirit to "proceed." In this evangelical perspective the addition of the *Filioque* simply reveals a total lack of understanding of the ontological signifiers, a transition to issues of a puerile religiosity. The monarchy of the Father is the only possibility of linguistic expression that identifies existence as regards origin with freedom rather than with necessity.

In *Person and Eros* I think I showed that the *monarchy of the Father* expresses the priority of freedom, that is, of persons, over against necessity, that is, over against essence (the definitive predetermination/fixed differentiation of personal existence). Naturally, in an ontological hermeneutics of this kind, the concept of *priority* can have neither a temporal nor an axiological significance. But this "naturally" (what is rationally self-evident) is not understood by those who, instead of alternative hermeneutic propositions, simply use labels (who characterize the priority of the person over against essence in a disdainful and dogmatic fashion without offering explanations: "personalism").

Let me also spell out the following: The falling away of the post-Roman West toward the "poverty" of Judaic monotheism was first denounced by Gregory Palamas, precisely because in the addition of the *Filioque*, he recognized a religious insistence on "Godhead" as the primary essential onticity. In his little book *On Being and Essence* (*De Esse et Essentia*), Thomas Aquinas presents this inability of the West from the outset (deriving from Augustine) to recognize in the priority of the person of the Father (a priority of Fatherhood, not of Godhead) the fundamental core of the Church's gospel.

Finally, in response to the last part of your question, I would not be so bold as to objectify by some linguistic expression in what way the Spirit, the Paraclete, differs from the Son. In the "Orthodox" "dogmatic" manuals that have been influenced by the West (those of a Western type and exhibiting a Western-religionized outlook), you will find such attempts, which, I think, cry out their inadequacy: "The Father, through the Son, in the Holy Spirit creates the world," or "The Son becomes incarnate at the good pleasure of the Father and through the energy of the Spirit," and so on, and so forth. Ecclesial experience, however, ventures to make references to the Uncreated in a manner not subject to linguistic definition only in the celebratory forms of expression of the poetry and hymnology of worship—in the hymns, for example, that we sing on the feast of Pentecost, or in the hymn "Heavenly King" that we pray every day. It is there that marks of the personal (hypostatic) otherness of the Holy Spirit, the Paraclete, suggest themselves without his existence and activity being individualized.

One last comment: ecclesial experience also witnesses to the Son, from the very beginning, as *Logos* of the Father. The word *"logos"* in Greek signifies in the first place the *form (eidos)* of an existent, its *manifestation* or *disclosure*. The form is always *referential*: it refers to (comes toward) the recipient of the disclosure and "tells" the recipient *what* that which is disclosed *is (ti esti)*. *Logos*, then, is the *truth* of the existent (*a + lēthē*—"non-oblivion"—being the root of *alētheia*, "truth"), as that is, as referentiality. But *logos* (rational capacity) is also the ability of the recipient of the disclosure/truth to appropriate the existential disclosure as image (*eikōn, eidos*, from *idein*, "to see") and to formulate it mentally (*en-nōi*), making it a concept (*ennoia*). By signifying the referentiality of the form and the capacity for its intellectual appropriation ("recognition" in Greek is *ana-gnōrisis*, "knowing again"), *logos* ends up being identified with the significance of *relation*, with relation being defined as *logos* and *logos* being identified as an event of relation—the *reality* of relation comes to be judged analogically (*ana-ton-logon*, "according to the *logos*"), and relation comes to differentiate the true *logos* from that which is hypothetical or an illusion.

The word *"Logos"* is assigned by the testimony of ecclesial experience to the Son with all the richness of meaning that its origin and use carries in Greek. The words that have been used, at least in the European languages, to translate the Greek *logos* (*"ratio," "reason," "raison,"* "word," *"Wort," "parole"*) convey a semantic content that is wholly fragmentary and therefore, in a subtle but vital way, alter the polysemantic unity of the Greek word.

In the Greek experience the Son, as "in the beginning" the *Logos* of the Father (Jn 1.1), is the disclosure of the Father, the referentiality of the Father "outside" the Godhead. He is the activated rationality (wisdom and beauty) of God's created things/creatures, the character of a personal act that is revealed in the *kosmos* (in Greek "world," carrying the sense of *kosmēma*, or "ordered beauty") of the creation of the universe. And he is God's intervention "in the flesh" in history, the historical person of the incarnate *Logos*, Jesus the Christ (or anointed) of God.

In my view the West's lapse into the *Filioque* (and persistence in it) is a result of a very low level of intellectual and linguistic culture. The persistence in it has been accompanied by an obstinacy resulting from a sense of inferiority.

Orthodoxy and the European Union

NR: *You have said that "Hellenism will not survive historically if it continues to fail to participate in the European process, if it remains on the margins of the changes that are taking place" (Kathēmerinē, December 18, 2011). The European Union is a Western European creation founded on Western European principles. Do traditionally Orthodox countries have a special difficulty in accommodating these principles?*

CY: They have a tremendous difficulty. The habituation of many, very many, centuries to priorities centered on the community, to the need for relations of communion, to the promotion of personal otherness, makes it almost impossible for Greek Orthodox to adapt to institutions founded on the West's individual-centered priorities, on the exaltation of "the rights of the individual," the autonomy of utilitarian rationalism in matters of organization, the independence of economics from the "community of use," the independence of politics from the communion of personal relations, and so on. From the foundation of the modern Greek state (1833) to the present day, nearly two hundred years later, we Greek-speaking citizens have attempts to become "Europeans," and we have failed to do so. The result is that we are now neither Greeks nor Europeans, but are trapped in a bastard kind of fourth-world underdevelopment.

If I insist that in spite of everything we should remain in the European Union, it is because I believe that Hellenism ceases to exist if it does not participate, as a proposition of culture, in the historical process. And it is only by participating in the contemporary global tragedy of the collapse of the Western cultural paradigm (of individualism and naturalism) can Hellenism, perhaps, reemerge from its habitual recycling of secondhand ideas and mimicking of the West and rediscover its historical role: to be the critic and creative challenger of the culture of the West.

I would venture to say that the manifest crisis of our striking— in terms of useful achievements—Western paradigm appears to be the end result, after a thousand years, of the consequences of the schism. The religionization of the ecclesial event in the then-barbarian West today constitutes a globalized one-way street. The symptoms of collapse are not only the alienation of faith/trust as ideology, the Vatican-like management of ideological "correctness" that gives birth to the nightmare of totalitarianism, and the version of "catholicity" as a geographical ubiquity that gives birth to the international ideologies of black and red fascism with the horror of the *Konzentrationlager* and the Gulag as applications of a "Holy Inquisition." Symptoms of the collapse of the Western paradigm are not only the independence today of the economy from relations of production and exchange, its transformation into a horrific game of international betting on the stock exchanges, the independence of politics from the community of citizens, and its transformation into an oligarchic tyranny not subject to democratic control.

The collapse becomes total as an absolute impasse, because there is no longer any institutional (i.e., belonging to the ecclesial body) opponent to the religionized Christianity that broke off in 1054 from the one catholic Church. Then the schismatics were a minority. Today religionization prevails in both East and West. Today even the Protestants and even the Orthodox have Vaticans, an ideological version of truth, a version of the Church as a form of organization with the aim of attaining an "efficiency" that "sanctifies" any "means" useful for imposing their authority.

I may be mistaken, but I believe that the testimony of ecclesial experience maintains its catholicity in scattered personal voices. Do read again T. S. Eliot's play *The Family Reunion*, and find me, if you can, a piece of writing by a patriarch, bishop, or theologian today with a comparable revelatory analysis of the lack of "meaning" that is guiding the Western paradigm to its historical end, the schism to its ultimate consequences.

The Church as Ecclesial Event

NR: *You have argued powerfully in your books for a Church that is not "religionized," not ideological, and not authoritarian—a Church that realizes the triadic mode of existence. What institutional expression of the ecclesial event meets these criteria?*

CY: I think that the answer to your question lies in the phrase from Luke's Gospel: "The Kingdom of God is not coming with things that can be observed; nor will they say, 'Look, here it is!' or 'There it is!' " (Lk 17.20–21). I believe that every institutional realization and manifestation of the Church is a historical failure—another of Christ's sayings compares the Church to a field of wheat in which weeds have also been sown, where they grow together until the harvest (Mt 13.24–30).

This growing together of wheat and weeds is a scandal to our logical minds and to our sensibilities. It is very painful for anyone to see (as I would suppose in every age) flourishing in the Church's institutional life (in the vast majority of the bishops, the clergy, and the laity) such gross ignorance of the Church's truth, of its goals, and of the *modes* and practice that make it *ecclēsia* and differentiate it from natural religion (from the religion of individualistic instincts and psychological urges). Yet since the Church *is* a historical failure, an institutional reality where alienation predominates the very cheapening of its experience and witness, and often its baseness and lust for power allows us to understand that which Christ revealed in Paul: "My power is made perfect in weakness" (2 Cor 12.9). If the historical ecclesiastical institutions had been "objectively" and demonstrably infallible, virtuous, and irreproachable, then the truth of the kingdom of God would have been identified with the idolization of the Church on earth, a version of it as an idealized "taboo." If everything within the institutional Church were to be imagined as accomplished and fully achieved—perfected virtue, holiness, and orthodox thinking—I, a sinner, would de facto be excluded from it; I would not dare to attempt to participate in it. On the other hand, when the knowledge prevails that the institutional Church on earth is an arena for athletic struggle where what is of first importance is not the setting of records, but the exercise of free choice and the awareness of our insufficicency, then from a need for the worship of idols and a fearful anxiety about our individual salvation, we pass to the joy of our inclusion within the communion of the beloved of the Father, of the brothers and sisters of the first-born in the new humanity of Jesus.

Sin, failure, and unworthiness do not threaten the ecclesial event. Only illusion threatens it, the distortion of its truth. And since ecclesial truth is not ideological, illusion is not the breaking of codified rules, the misinterpretation and corruption of "convictions"; it is the Church's alienation in practice into a religion, an ideology, a moral system, a pietism, a psychological consolation, a mark of nationalism, and a heritage.

I believe that we shall not find the Church's truth in some institutional expression of it. It will be granted to us, if we are found worthy of it "as in a mirror, dimly," personally, like every important discovery in our lives. The way we discover it will be different for each one of us—perhaps in some pages of the Fathers; in liturgical experiences; in the impact on us of a piece of architecture; in hearing some music; in "passing over" through art "to the prototype"; in parish meetings; in theological studies; or in "encounters" with saints, either living or long since dead. "The kingdom of God is as if someone would scatter seed on the ground, and would sleep and rise night and day, and the seed would sprout and grow, he does not know how. The earth produces of itself . . ." (Mk 4.26–28).

What is particularly painful is the insistence, for a thousand years now, on an "infallible cathedra" and on an almost automatic canonization of each deceased pope—an insistence on the triumph of the religionization of the ecclesial event as the foundation of a globalized culture.

NR: *In your account of your time with the Zoe movement, you castigate the Western ideological (mainly Protestant) ideas that pervaded the thinking of the cadres. Yet the first breath of change came through the informal teaching of Koutroubis, who brought knowledge of de Lubac, Daniélou, Congar, Bouyer, and others of the* "nouvelle théologie" *current (inspired by the Greek Fathers) that was beginning to transform the way theology was being approached in France. It was also through Koutroubis, who had studied with the Jesuits, that the name of Gregory Palamas became known again in Greece. The relationship between Greek theology and the West is a complex one, isn't it? It is not simply a matter of "them" and "us." The cross-fertilization has been valuable in both directions.*

CY: I don't know if the relationship between ecclesial Orthodoxy and the religionized West is all that complicated. At any rate, in my own eyes this relationship was never one of ideological rivalry. In the preface to the French edition of *The Freedom of Morality* (Labor et Fides, 1982), I think I was able to express adequately enough what I experienced personally of this relationship—I would very much like you to read this piece. My time in the pietistic Zoe movement helped me to understand experientially that not every erroneous version of ecclesial witness (in teaching, practice, worship, or organization) leads simply to mistaken convictions, or to an alienation of the form of the Liturgy, or to more autocratic forms of administration. No. Error in the way the Church's witness is appropriated generates sickness, interior impoverishment, psychological distortions—that is to say, unhappiness and torment. The bipolar schema of truth/falsity refers to life itself, not to convictions or conduct. It is realized as health or sickness. When, for example, sin is understood as *guilt*, rather than (as the Church teaches) as *failure/missing-the-mark*, it generates a guilty conscience, a typical mark of the Western person, a sickness and torment that afflicts him or her. Augustine's legalism is the "practical" side of the religionization of the Church in the post-Roman West that generated the "logistical" version of confession, the tyrannical authority exercised by the clergy, the notorious "indulgences," and finally the nightmare of Protestant ethics. A guilty conscience is lifelong. It endures day and night, a torment to human beings, an enslavement to pangs and fears, a poisonous secretion of the super-ego that stifles every joy. Sin is experienced as self-depreciation, as confinement within the egocentricity of the pangs of a wounded egoism.

The same is true for the understanding of *askēsis* as a legal obligation, and therefore as an egotistic attainment of measurable grades of achievement of a competitive character. This also leads inevitably to narcissism as a psychological illness—individuals see their ego as an erotic object and find themselves unable in reality to love anything that is not themselves. Individual salvation and its attainment (namely, that the atomic ego should exist in endless linear time) becomes a fixed idea that imprisons both existence and conduct. People see everywhere around the possible pollution of their "purity," and therefore constant threats that undermine their ego, that pose a risk to their self-esteem.

Error in the appropriation of ecclesial truth generates illness and existential alienation, not simply as faulty perceptions or "principles." A glaring example is the insistence of Roman Catholicism on the obligatory celibacy of all the clergy and the insistence of Orthodoxism on the obligatory celibacy of the episcopate and of widowed presbyters. How much illness has been generated by this insistence, this impalement on the authoritarian and sadomasochistic intentionalities that dictate it! How much perversion; how much dramatic surrender to unnatural licentiousness; how many tragedies destructive of human existences; how much pharisaical concealment of condoned crimes, intellectual eunuchism, and unloving, private lasciviousness! An erroneous appropriation or deliberate distortion of the Church's gospel leads inexorably to a pathogenic situation, to the tormenting of humankind.

To return to your point, of course Daniélou, de Lubac, Congar, and Bouyer helped my generation to rediscover the Fathers of the undivided Church, to appreciate the poverty and sterility of "Orthodox" writings on dogmatics by Christos Androutsos, Philaret of Moscow, Platon of Moscow, and Panayiotis Trembelas—the blind alleys of academic Orthodoxism, of an unconscious but radical Westernization of what was once the Church's witness. At that time, in the 1960s and 1970s, we believed that this unexpected "turn" by the above group of exceptionally talented Roman Catholic theologians toward the Greek Fathers of the Church was also influencing Catholicism's leadership and, specifically, the decisions of the Second Vatican Council that was then being held (1962–65).

Disappointment came gradually but in the end was complete and irreversible. I remember in 1992, when the official *Catechism* of the Roman Catholic Church was published, that is to say, the official formulation of its teaching, a work authored or edited by Joseph Ratzinger, later Pope Benedict XVI, I perused its pages and almost collapsed. First, the character of the work was very clearly and self-evidently ideological—the turning of the Church's witness into an ideology that was accomplished by the scholastic theologians of the Middle Ages and was imposed down the centuries without any protest. *Faith* for the West continues to be not a *mode* of existence, but a set of atomic convictions that are received intellectually. Second, within this ideologized presentation, which makes absolutes of the "noumenal" and excludes the *mode*, room was very easily found for what in our own days has been considered an identity marker of the Orthodox Catholic Church: for example, quotations from the Greek Fathers, references to theology's apophaticism, to eucharistic ecclesiology, to a personalist ontology. When Roman Catholicism has been turned into an ideological construct, it finds room for anything.

This mirrors precisely the way the theology of the Russian diaspora or the blood and torture of the martyrs of the Russian Church in the period of communist tyranny were unable to produce the slightest crack in the hardened religionization of the Patriarchate of Moscow, in its undisguised thirst for worldly power, for a return to the tsarist period of megalomania. Exactly the same was the case with the Orthodoxism of the Greek state as regards any influence exercised on it by the theological and monastic sectors at the time of the so-called "generation of the '60s."

The opposition is not between "Orthodoxy" and the "West," but between individualistic "religion" and ecclesial communion, between the wheat and the tares that grow together in the field of historical experience. It seems that in our era it is the tares that prevail completely, the ignorance of the "mode," the one-way street of the atomic *cogito*, of the atomic *desidero*—the two elements that mark the identity of the Western "paradigm." For each of us to be born, however, to enter into existence, no decision was taken by our individual intellect, nor was it desired by our individual will. We needed a father, a mother, and their love—that is the "mode" by which existence is realized. We did not come from our thinking or from our "unfettered" will. Thus for us also to be born into the "mode" of the uncreated, into freedom from any predetermination and necessity of existence, we need a father/bishop and a mother/eucharistic community. And we need our love—this is the "mode" of entry into the kingdom, into existential freedom. It is that we should exist because we want to exist, and that we should want to exist because we love. Infants at the beginning, we neither understand the goal properly, nor do we desire it with any clarity. The comparison Paul makes applies to us literally: "When I was a child, I spoke as a child, I behaved as a child, I thought as a child. But when I became an adult I put away childish things" (1 Cor 13.11). And elsewhere he concludes, "Therefore not from the will, nor from circumstances, but from God in his mercy" (Rom 9.16).

Our effort should be to surrender to his love, free from servitude to the *cogito* and the *desidero*, to believe in him, which means: to trust in his manic love. For many centuries two "paradigms" have existed on the stage of history: the individualistic cultural "paradigm," which was generated by the religionization of the ecclesial event in the post-Roman barbarian West; and the communitarian "paradigm" of the Greek *polis* and the ecclesial Eucharist. Today the Western "paradigm" has acquired a global reach and dominates the whole planet (it has swallowed up not only the Hellenic culture that was its deadly rival, obliterating the Greek *polis* and the eucharistic community, but also other communitarian civilizations of great antiquity: those of China, Tibet, and India). Our faith is severely tested, because in the field of history we now see only tares—there is no wheat for us to ascertain the difference.

NR: *In* Against Religion *you lament the way Orthodox patriarchates have become multiplied along national lines. In the late sixteenth century, Moscow attained patriarchal status, perhaps in connection with the "Third Rome" ideology current at that time. Other countries with majority Orthodox populations became patriarchates later with the rise of nationalism in the nineteenth century. What is the ecclesiological role of a patriarchate?*

CY: This is a question, my dear Norman, that I believe should be addressed today by an ecumenical council. The word "patriarchate," after Moscow's licentious act, is empty of any ecclesiological content. It simply stands for an administrative unit, autonomous and independent, within a system of coexisting but synodically uncommunicating ethnicities, which are "autocephalous" in their "religious" life.

A historical investigation that I believe should precede discussion in an ecumenical council is the following: How and why did the recognition of a *metropolis* ("mother-city") as a *patriarchate* come to be linked to the political ambition of an ethnicity to form an *empire*? I am referring to the cases of the Bulgarian leader Symeon (890–927), the Serb Stephen Dušan (1308–55), and the ambition of Moscow to be recognized as a Third Rome in succession to the Roman Empire. If we study the reasons (at all events secular and not in the least ecclesial) for the creation of the semantic correlation between the terms "empire" and "patriarchate," perhaps we shall find some justification for the modern (since the nineteenth century) comical demand of every ethnicity that constitutes an independent, self-governing state to change the title of the bishops who presides over the synod of local bishops to "patriarch."

The topic is a sad and painful one, because it reveals the undisguised and unhesitating alienation of the ecclesial event into a national "religion," the institutionalized abandonment of *ecclesiology*, that is, of the truth about the Church and its gospel to which experiential witness has been given. The now well-established ethnophyletic "patriarchates" and the equally autonomous and ethnophyletic *autocephalous churches*, which have been detached from the ancient patriarchates, presuppose and by their institutional existence confirm that the cohesion of Christians on the international level is chiefly or exclusively ideological (Christians simply coincide in the formalistic acceptance of common convictions—commonly obligatory "dogmas" and, in part, common "canons," that is, legal precepts). We can only speak conventionally about *synodical* and *liturgical* cohesion, since the institution of a synod or council is understood only in administrative terms as an institution concerning the internal affairs of each national (ethnophyletic) church. Fortunately, "inter-Orthodox" or even "Panorthodox" meetings of official representatives" (not only of bishops) of the national churches are simply called "consultations." And they function self-evidently as arenas for shabby rivalries over jurisdictional claims of a worldly character, for asserting or disputing "primacies of honor," and for strengthening collective or individual egos.

It seems to have been completely forgotten or to have been systematically ignored that "patriarchate," together with "metropolis," is an empty word without the operation of the synodical system; they are titles cut off from their function, *nomina nuda*. We have forgotten—we are in a state of ignorance that has lasted for centuries—that a synod or council is an extension of the

Eucharist, that just as when the Eucharist is concelebrated, one celebrant presides, in the image of the monarchy of the Father, the same is the case at a synod. For in the Church everything functions by realizing the "mode" of true life, of the triadic *perichōrēsis* of existence and operation. Consequently, that which is atomic or individual—will, energy, virtue—is reliance on the *mode* of the created, of existential failure, a reliance on death.

NR: *It seems increasingly anomalous that the ecumenical patriarch should be residing in a city, modern Istanbul, that has now only a miniscule Christian population. Sensible voices say that he should move his seat to a more Orthodox environment, perhaps to Mount Athos or the United States. And yet . . . I must confess to an intense nostalgia for Christian Constantinople. The Phanar for me is full of associations, personal as well as historical. I have a vivid memory of myself as a seventeen-year-old visiting the great Patriarch Athenagoras with my younger sister and being enveloped by him in a fatherly embrace. "You are my spiritual grandchildren," he said. If the patriarch were to leave the Phanar, would that not be a symbolic validation of Moscow as the "Third Rome," not to mention an abandonment of the patriarch's historic role?*

CY: Nostalgic memories, my dear Norman, and sentimental attachments are precious elements in the personal life of each of us, but they do not have vital significance for the sense we make of the function of the Ecumenical Patriarchate. The fact alone that the Ecumenical Patriarchate is the only institutional possibility that remains to us for the realization and manifestation of the unity/cohesion of the catholic Church "throughout the oecumene" gives it a unique value that is very precious.

If I have understood it correctly, in the Church there are no high offices (*axiōmata*); there are only official functions (*leitourgēmata*) and the value of the functionaries is measured by the criterion of self-transcendence and self-offering. "He who wishes to be first must be the servant of all." The primacy of Constantinople is a primacy of responsibility, a cross-bearing service. He is the only bishop (deciding and acting synodically) who has the power to convoke an ecumenical council.

In the Church, if I have understood it correctly, quantity is never a measure or criterion of primacy, precedence, or leadership. The patriarchates are not evaluated in accordance with the population they serve, the geographical extent of their jurisdiction or the economic means at their disposal. They are evaluated in accordance with their contribution to the realization and manifestation of the truth of the Church. Rome, Constantinople, Alexandria, and Antioch are each to this day a specific contribution to the *mode* that constitutes the Church—a mode of theology, worship, and iconography, ways of realizing and manifesting the ecclesial "mode" of each one. Even Jerusalem, as the *topos* or place of the incarnate manifestation of God serves the *ou-topia*, or nonlocalization, of the "mode." It manifests, illuminates, and proclaims the ecclesial "mode" in the historical place where it was first revealed.

If the consciousness of these fundamental presuppositions were established universally, it would have been self-evident by now that the Ecumenical Patriarchate of Constantinople should be freed from the servitude of remaining in a country and among a population hostile to the Christian gospel and should move to the former imperial co-capital (*Symbasileuousa polis*) of Thessalonica, retaining the title and responsibilities (the historical continuity) of its Hellenic ecumenicity. But the subjection today of the so-called "Orthodox" churches to the mentality and blinkered self-interest of ethnicities does not permit the risk, the risk of casting doubt on the last remaining guarantee of the unity of the catholic Church throughout the *oikoumenē*. Remaining in a country belonging to people of a different faith and hostile to the

Church protects the Hellenic ecumenicity of the Patriarchate of Constantinople from becoming subject to Greek nationalism or to being disputed as a Greek national institution by malevolent denigrators. The Ecumenical Patriarchate's flock is Hellenism's ecumenical diaspora, not the provincial Greek population of the southern tip of the Balkans.

NR: *You mention the special role of Jerusalem. Since Ottoman times the Confraternity of the Holy Sepulchre has controlled election to the Patriarchate of Jerusalem. Throughout the twentieth century the history of the patriarchate is a sad one, with Greek interests dedicating much of their effort to prevent the "Arabization" of the Orthodox Church of Jerusalem. It seems to me that this effort to preserve a Greek presence has been detrimental to the Orthodox—the opportunity of the patriarch to be a true father to the Orthodox faithful has been squandered. Are there any more hopeful signs for the twenty-first century?*

CY: Let us not forget the tragedy that Hellenism has lived through for the past 190 years, that is to say, from the time of the foundation of the Greek national state in the south of the Balkan Peninsula in 1822. Until that time, until the proclamation at the First National Assembly at Epidaurus on January 1, 1822, "before God and men"—a proclamation "of the political existence and independence of the Hellenic nation, which has shaken off the cruel and unprecedented yoke of tyranny under the frightful rule of the Ottomans"—until that time, what were Hellenism's geographical boundaries? From 2000 BC, when archeologists have verified that there were twenty-two Greek tribes established or wandering as nomads in an area extending from present-day Croatia to Cape Tainaron (the southernmost point of mainland Greece), and in Crete, the littoral of Asia Minor, the Aegean Archipelago, and Cyprus, with a common language, a common technique of toolmaking, jewelery, and ceramics—from that time until the Assembly at Epidaurus in 1822, where was Hellenism to be located in geographical terms? Odysseas Elytis affirms with good reason that "however strange it may seem, before the two world wars a subject of the microscopic [Greek] state [still] breathed the air of roughly a single empire. His ability to move about without any change of language covered large areas of Italy and Austria, the whole of Egypt, southern Bulgaria, Romania, the Russian Caucasus and, naturally, Constantinople and its hinterland along the whole length of the Aegean Coast, what we call today south-west Turkey."

For about four millennia Hellenism was a "mode" of life, a language, an art, a metaphysical quest—a mode without frontiers, because it concerned humanity as a whole. Without frontiers, but with a clear identity and very specific provenance. After the campaigns of Alexander the Great, the Greek "mode" was internationalized; it became "ecumenical," that is, self-evidently belonging to all humanity, a cosmopolitan culture in the root sense of the word. And thanks to the reception of Christianity by the peoples of the Hellenized Roman "*oikoumenē*," the Church's gospel came to embody the dynamic of globalism.

By this historical summary, what I want to say is that Hellenicity is the only possible way the ancient Patriarchates of Jerusalem or Alexandria have of really remaining supranational, not subject to provincialism, narrow-mindedness, and ethnic self-interest, but ecclesially ecumenical. Unfortunately, the Patriarchate of Jerusalem is staffed mainly by people from Greece, men as a rule of very humble background, chiefly from the islands of Samos and Chios. They live in the distinguished Jerusalem environment of Hellenic cosmopolitanism, but their reflexes and their mentality are those of a provincial Greek nationalism.

That is why they are afraid of the Arab population that constitutes the lay body, today's historical flesh of the patriarchate. If they understood that Hellenicity, that is, ecumenicity, is not located in blood, in biological descent, but in the cultivation of self-denial with the aim of serving high goals of universal human relevance, they would have persuaded the Arab Orthodox of what is self-evident: that if the patriarchate becomes Greek or Arabic, it will expire in the poverty of a provincial nationalism. It will be able to become again a living pivot of ecclesial catholicity only if it recovers its Hellenic cosmopolitanism.

The Challenge of Islam

NR: *The violent events in London and Paris in recent years have thrown a spotlight on the resentments of marginalized young Muslims in Western Europe—exacerbated in France, perhaps, by the strong French emphasis on* laïcité. *How is a thoughtful Christian to respond to a resurgent (and often radicalized) Islam?*

CY: The astonishing dynamics that Islam manifests in our day is a large and important subject. It would do it an injustice to deal with it in a summary fashion. Let me just offer one thought as a challenge for our topic.

I think that the triumphant spread of Islam on our planet, and especially the conversion of indigenous Western Europeans to this religion, is perhaps a result of the globalization of a *mode* of life (a "paradigm") that imposes as the unique "meaning" (cause and purpose) of human existence the *maximalization of consumer convenience*. Consumer convenience tends to be the only or chief joy of human beings today, the measure of their *quality* of life.

As an absolutely individualist pursuit/delight/goal, consumption gives specific tangible flesh to the (originally religious) individualism that imposed itself on the post-Roman West, drawing its "authority" from Augustine. The reliance on an individualistic "salvation" always presupposed privations, anxious guilt, and subjection to regulative principles. The individualism of historical materialism (Marxism and capitalism) is hedonistic, and therefore invincible. Roman Catholic moralistic legalism and Protestant puritanism-pietism have for centuries preached a disembodied, abstract "salvation" at the cost of a masochistic individualism. The Enlightenment brought to the West a thoroughly consistent individualism, an affirmation of the transient, but an affirmation that is strikingly pleasurable, graspable, and intoxicating.

The "salvation" proclaimed by the Enlightenment has tangible historical flesh: the guaranteeing of individual rights; freedom as the unrestricted power of the individual to make choices; and an astonishing technology in the service of the well-being, sovereignty, imposition, convenience, and pleasurable satiety of the individual. Of course, this tangible "salvation" has been accompanied by lack of "meaning," by the nullification of any "value" transcending time and decay.

The natural individualistic need to escape from the closed, claustrophobic horizon of nihilism leads inexorably to an (almost involuntary) slide into any kind of blind, irrational-but-practical "faith." The pure-born Englishman with his cultured voice that the whole world saw beheading his fellow human beings with utter dispassion in front of the camera is a thoroughly consistent fruit of the West's contemporary nihilism. He converted to Islam believing he was fighting the emptiness in his soul by surrendering himself to a hallucinatory, blind faith.

Islam presents a fruitful challenge to our Christianity. At least it should make us aware that an individualistic (rather than empirically shared ecclesial) "faith" generates terror and creates monsters.

The Scope of Yannaras's Work

NR: *In recent years you have embarked on an ambitious program of presenting your books in translation, not only in English and other Western European languages, but also in the Slavic languages and Romanian. What are you hoping to achieve?*

CY: I would not describe it as a "program." For many years now, I have wanted some of my books to be translated into other languages because, quite frankly, I longed for a critique, for my work to be evaluated in a way that is impossible in Greece. Greece today is a country in which no one is ever offered constructive criticism on anything. Nobody and nothing—from books, scientific research and art, to politics and management of the economy—is ever evaluated impartially. It is perhaps the characteristic mark of the decadence into which Hellenism has fallen. Whatever reviews appear in periodicals, newspapers, or television shows, as a rule they are either publicity puffs or ideological attacks where the reviewer seeks to put down his or her rival.

If my work, for several decades now, has built up a proposal for an "ontology of the person"—whether adequate or inadequate, whether coherent or arbitrary and mistaken, but at any rate a proposal put forward to provoke dialogue (since it sets the issue of ontology on a new basis and in various separate studies tests this proposal in the fields of ethics, epistemology, law, and political economy)—then there has never been in Greece even one attempt at a critique, positive or negative, of this proposal. There has only been a half-page footnote in an article of 1977 by John Zizioulas that axiomatically rejects *Person and Eros* because, supposedly, "it uses Heidegger to justify patristic theology"!

Whatever personal attempts I have made to have my books translated into other European languages have all met with failure. Those books that have been translated and published were always unexpected surprises, evidence of an interest I had not anticipated. I approached a large number of publishers with a view to having translations published in English but received rejections from all of them. Finally, without my expecting it, I received the gift of an excellent translator and a publisher—Holy Cross Orthodox Press—who have to date brought out eight of my books in English.

Of course, the critique has yet to appear, but at least the challenge has been issued on a broader linguistic stage.

NR: *You have noted that Trembelas worked in isolation, attracted no disciples, and was not concerned to leave any heirs. Who do you see continuing your own work?*

CY: The comment I made on Trembelas specifically concerned his successors in his university chair. That there should be a successor or successors to a writer's inquiries and issues that he or she treats is something that is perhaps not subject to a program. The coincidence or coordination of interests emerges, is born—it cannot be planned and prepared in advance.

I very much want the questions that for me remain open to be addressed by others in the future and for them to be granted that indescribable joy that accompanies the gift of answers—that they can be accommodated in language, or simply in the acceptance that some of the things that are essential cannot be said in words.

Prosopography

Afanassieff, Nicolas (1893–1966). Professor of canon law and the history of the early Church at the Theological Institute of St Sergius in Paris from 1930 to 1966. Afanassieff was a pioneer of the eucharistic ecclesiology later developed by John Zizioulas and others.

Agouridis, Savvas (1921–2007). Professor of New Testament exegesis at the University of Thessalonica from 1950 until 1970, when he moved to take up a similar post at the University of Athens. Opposition to his modernism forced him to retire prematurely. He nevertheless continued to hold seminars in which he trained many of the exegetes who hold teaching positions today in Greek universities.

Alcuin (ca. 740–804). An English ecclesiastical scholar at the court of Charlemagne, who contributed significantly to the Carolingian intellectual renaissance.

Allchin, A. M. (Donald) (1930–2010). Anglican priest and theologian with a deep feeling for Orthodoxy. He was a leading member of the Fellowship of St Alban and St Sergius, a residentiary canon of Canterbury Cathedral, and the warden, successively, of two Anglican religious communities.

Ambrose of Milan (339–97), St. Born in Augusta Treverorum (Trier), the son of the praetorian prefect of Gaul, he was elected bishop of Milan in 373 or 374, even though he was still an unbaptized layman. One of the greatest of the early Fathers, he was a strong opponent of Arianism and a rigorous upholder of the value of consecrated virginity.

Anagnostopoulos, Georgios. Orthodox priest and professor in the Electrical and Computer Engineering Department of the Democritus University of Thrace, with an expertise in space electrodynamics.

Androutsos, Christos (1867–1935). Professor of dogmatics and Christian ethics at the University of Athens from 1912 to shortly before his death, Androutsos exercised an enormous influence in the Orthodox world through his *Dogmatics of the Eastern Orthodox Church* (Athens, 1907). Trained in Germany (at the University of Leipzig), his approach was strongly rationalistic, with little influence from the patristic tradition.

Anselm of Canterbury (ca. 1033–1109). An Italian by birth, he became abbot of the Norman abbey of Bec and then, in 1093, archbishop of Canterbury. The most distinguished Western philosopher and theologian between Augustine and Aquinas, he developed the ontological argument for the existence of God and a doctrine of atonement that laid emphasis on satisfaction for sin.

Athenagoras I (1886–1972). Ecumenical patriarch from 1948 to 1972. Before becoming patriarch, he was Greek archbishop of North and South America (1930–48), where he healed a schism that had long troubled the archdiocese. Always a peacemaker, he sought to bring the autocephalous Orthodox churches closer together and also to encourage cooperation between Christians generally. His most memorable achievement was his meeting in Jerusalem in 1964 with Pope Paul VI, which resulted a year later in the lifting of the anathemas of 1054, though this was not well received by many Orthodox in Greece.

Augustine of Hippo (354–430). Born in Thagaste (in modern Algeria) to a pagan father and Christian mother, Augustine was baptized by St Ambrose in 387 and was made bishop of Hippo Regius in 391. Particularly noted for his sensitive spiritual introspection and his teaching on humanity's fallen state, his many writings have made him not only the greatest of the Latin Fathers, but also a towering figure in the Western intellectual tradition as a whole.

Balthasar, Hans Urs von (1905–88). Swiss Jesuit whose enormous output included important works on the Fathers. His *Kosmische Liturgie* (1941) laid the basis for modern study of St Maximus the Confessor. A great theologian, he was named a cardinal in 1988 by Pope John Paul II but died before the red hat could be conferred.

Bartholomew I (1940–). Ecumenical patriarch since 1991, Bartholomew I is a church leader of high international stature. He has expended much effort on inter-Orthodox cooperation, a vital task since the disintegration of the Soviet bloc, and has also been prominent in interfaith dialogue. He is known widely outside the Orthodox Church for his promotion of religious freedom and human rights and his work in the fields of ecology and the protection of the environment.

Berdyaev, Nicolas (1874–1948). A Russian religious philosopher from an old noble family who settled in France after being expelled from Russia in 1922. He established an academy of philosophy and religion in Paris, where he taught and wrote. His numerous books have been widely translated. Among the most influential have been *Freedom and the Spirit* (London, 1935), *The Destiny of Man* (London, 1937), and *The Russian Idea* (London, 1947).

Bobrinskoy, Boris (1925–). Professor of dogmatic theology at the Theological Institute of St Sergius in Paris from 1954 to 2006, and honorary dean of the St Sergius. Fr Bobrinskoy has published many books on the Liturgy, the Holy Spirit, and the Church. He is also a well-known broadcaster and has taken an active part in the ecumenical movement.

Bouyer, Louis (1913–2004). Catholic theologian of the period of renewal before and after the Second Vatican Council. Ordained a Lutheran pastor in 1936, he was received into the Catholic Church in 1944 (having considered Orthodoxy on the way). He then joined the Oratorians and was for many years a professor at the Institut Catholique in Paris. He was a consultant for the Liturgy at Vatican II and served on several international commissions. An expert on patristic and later Orthodox spiritual teaching, his writings are of lasting value.

Bradshaw, David. A professor of philosophy at the University of Kentucky, Bradshaw is the author of the much-discussed book *Aristotle East and West: Metaphysics and the Division of Christendom* (Cambridge, 2004), notable for its defense of the Palamite synthesis.

Bulgakov, Sergius (1871–1944). One of the most profound Orthodox theologians of the twentieth century, Bulgakov began his career as a Marxist professor of political economy at Kiev. He returned to the Church in the period of the "Russian religious renaissance" and was ordained a priest in 1918. In 1922 he was one of the intellectuals whom Lenin exiled from Russia. When he arrived in Paris, Metropolitan Evlogy (Georgievsky) invited him to become professor of dogmatic theology at the newly established Institute of St Sergius. He remained there until his death, despite the controversy surrounding him over his sophiology, that is, his doctrine of divine wisdom. An English translation of his great dogmatic trilogy, written in Russian in the 1930s, has only been published in this century: *The Bride of the Lamb* (Grand

Rapids, MI, 2002), *The Comforter* (Grand Rapids, MI, 2004), and *The Bride of the Lamb* (Grand Rapids, MI, 2008).

Cavafy, C. P. (1863–1933). Greek poet of Alexandria whose remarkable combination of philosophical, historical, and hedonistic themes in an idiom drawing on all registers of the Greek language inaugurated a new era in Greek poetry. His complete poems have been published in several English translations.

Chenu, Marie-Dominique (1895–1990). Dominican priest and pioneer of the movement of *ressourcement*, the recovery of a historical (as opposed to a purely intellectualist) approach to theology. He completed his doctorate in Rome on Thomas Aquinas under Reginald Garrigou-Lagrange but became dissatisfied with the latter's neo-Thomist approach. He came under official censure for his opinions, and his teaching career was accordingly curtailed, but eventually he was vindicated and invited as a *peritus* (theological expert) to the Second Vatican Council.

Chitty, Derwas J. (1901–71). Anglican priest, the rector of a country parish (Upton Parva in Oxfordshire) for thirty-seven years, who was a distinguished student of early monasticism. He was a leading member of the Fellowship of St Alban and St Sergius. His main publication, *The Desert a City* (London, 1966), on the origins of monasticism in Egypt and Palestine, remains a classic.

Clément, Olivier (1921–2009). French Orthodox writer and theologian who did much to make Orthodoxy known to a broad public in France. Brought up in a nonreligious family, he embraced Orthodoxy at the age of thirty through his reading of Berdyaev and Lossky. In 1959 he became editor of *Contacts*, and three years later was appointed professor of comparative and moral theology at the Institute of St Sergius. A warm personality, he enjoyed friendships with many prominent Christians, including

Patriarch Athenagoras I, the Romanian theologian Dumitru Stǎniloae, Pope John Paul II, and Brother Roger of Taizé.

Congar, Yves Marie-Joseph (1904–95). Dominican priest who emphasized the role of the laity in the Church and was an important figure in the movement for reform before the Second Vatican Council. His enthusiasm for the ecumenical movement (expressed in his first book, *Chrétiens désunis* [Paris, 1937]) and his ideas for reform in the Roman Catholic Church (set out in *Vraie et fausse réforme dans l'Église* [Paris, 1950]), resulted in disciplinary measures being imposed on him by Rome, which silenced him for many years. But the latter book impressed Angelo Roncalli, who became Pope John XXIII. When Pope John summoned the Second Vatican Council, Congar was invited to participate as a theological expert. Seven months before his death, he was made a cardinal.

Daniélou, Jean (1905–74). Jesuit priest who played an important part in the renewal of Catholic theology in the twentieth century through *ressourcement*, or going back to the sources. He was one of the founders in 1942 of Sources chrétiennes, a series of volumes of patristic texts with French translations on the facing page. His doctoral thesis on St Gregory of Nyssa, published as *Platonisme et la théologie mystique* (Paris, 1944), inaugurated the modern Catholic study of the Fathers. Invited as a *peritus* (theological expert) to the Second Vatican Council, he was created a cardinal by Paul VI in 1969.

Descartes, René (1596–1650). French philosopher and mathematician whose method of systematic doubt replaced the scholasticism dominant in the Middle Ages and inaugurated the modern age in philosophy. His famous first principle of knowledge, *cogito ergo sum* ("I think, therefore I am"), laid the foundations of modern subjective rationalism.

Dostoevsky, Feodor (1821–1881). The greatest Russian novelist of the great age of Russian fiction. In his novels (*Crime and Punishment* [1866], *The Idiot* [1869], *The Devils* [1872], and *The Brothers Karamazov* [1880]), Orthodox Christianity does not simply provide a background for the stories, but permeates all the moral, philosophical, and religious issues that are treated in them. He was close to the Slavophiles, who saw Roman Catholicism as a secularized version of Christianity obsessed with the exercise of power.

Dragoumis, Ion (1878–1920). Greek diplomat, politician, and anti-irredentist nationalist. He was an opponent of the leader of the Greek liberals, Eleutherios Venizelos, who wanted to enlarge the borders of the Greek state at the expense of the Ottoman Empire. Dragoumis's vision of Hellenism was not based on the acquisition of territory. He saw the Greeks as becoming the leading economic and cultural force in the relatively secularized Ottoman Empire that resulted from the Young Turk revolution of 1908.

Duby, Georges (1919–96). Great French medieval historian who changed our perception of the Middle Ages by his emphasis on social history and its relationship with art. For most of his life, he was a professor at Aix-en-Provence. From 1970 to 1991, he was also professor of the history of medieval societies at the College de France in Paris.

Duquoc, Christian (1926–2008). A Dominican priest, Fr Duquoc served for many years (from 1956) as a professor at the Catholic University of Lyon. He was the author of numerous books on Christ, the Church, and the nature of Christian faith.

Eliot, T. S. (1888–1965). American-born English poet, playwright, and literary critic who exercised a profound influence on twentieth-century poetry in the English-speaking world and beyond. His Anglo-Catholic (high-church Anglican) faith provided him with a nonsentimental religious frame of reference in his poetry, particularly evident in *The Waste Land* (1922), *Ash Wednesday* (1930), and *Four Quartets* (1943). While he was an editor at the London publishers Faber and Faber, he commissioned the first publication of selections of the *Philokalia*, translated by E. Kadloubovsky and G. E. H. Palmer. He was awarded the Nobel Prize for Literature in 1948.

Elytis, Odysseas (1911–96). Greek lyrical poet and essayist who was a major exponent of romantic modernism. In 1979 he won the Nobel Prize for Literature (the only Greek to have done so to date, apart from his friend George Seferis) and declared in his acceptance speech that he wrote "in a tradition that has gone on since the time of Homer, in the embrace of Western civilization." He also declared himself "an idolator who, without wanting to do so, arrives at Christian sainthood." His *oeuvre* has been published in English translation as *The Collected Poems of Odysseus Elytis* (Baltimore, 1997).

Ephraim Katounakiotis (1912–98). A monk of the hermitage of Katounakia on Mount Athos for sixty-five years, Fr Ephraim was a well-known hesychast with the gift of clairvoyance and discernment.

Erickson, John H. (1943–). Professor emeritus of Church history at St Vladimir's Orthodox Seminary in New York, and dean of that institution from 2002 to 2007. A specialist in Eastern canon law, Fr Erickson is the author of many books and articles on the contemporary problems faced by the Orthodox Church.

Evdokimov, Michel (1930–). Son of Paul Evdokimov and French archpriest in the exarchate of the Patriarchate of Constantinople. An expert on Dostoevsky, he teaches in Paris at the Collège des Bernardins. Of his many books, his *Father Alexander Men:*

Martyr of Atheism (Leominster, 2011) has been translated into English.

Evdokimov, Paul (1901–70). Orthodox lay theologian. On leaving Russia in the aftermath of the revolution, Evdokimov settled in Paris, where he studied with Berdyaev and Bulgakov and was one of the founding members of the Russian Christian Student Movement. He became professor of moral theology at the Institute of St Sergius and also taught at the Institut Catholique. His work in the ecumenical movement led to a period as director of the Ecumenical Institute in Geneva and to his invitation to the Second Vatican Council as an Orthodox observer. Many of his books focus on the vocation of laypeople in the Church.

Every, George (1909–2003). Roman Catholic Byzantine scholar. From 1929 to 1973 Every was a member of an Anglican religious community, the Society of the Sacred Mission, at Kelham in England. There he came to know T. S. Eliot, a frequent visitor, whom he introduced to the church of Little Gidding. In 1973 he became a Roman Catholic and taught for a number of years at Oscott, the seminary of the Roman Catholic archdiocese of Birmingham. With Kallistos Ware and Robert Murray, he edited the *Eastern Churches Review* until its demise in 1978.

Florovsky, Georges (1893–1979). The most influential Orthodox theologian of the twentieth century. Born in Odessa, Florovsky left Russia after the revolution, eventually arriving in Paris. In 1925 he was appointed professor of patristics at the newly founded Institute of St Sergius, and in 1932 was ordained to the priesthood. In 1939 he was transferred to the chair of dogmatics, which he held for ten years. In 1949 he moved to the United States to become dean of St Vladimir's Seminary in New York. Asked to resign in 1955—he did not work easily with colleagues—he went on to become a professor at Harvard and then at Princeton. His "neopatristic synthesis" dominated twentieth-century Orthodox theology. The Greek Fathers defined Orthodoxy for him, not just as historical figures, but as witnesses to Christian truth; returning to "the mind of the Fathers" was the only way to heal Christian divisions. In his magnum opus, *Ways of Russian Theology* (Belmont, MA, 1979), originally published in Russian in 1937, he maintained that Western influences had led Russian theology, since the time of Peter the Great, into a "Babylonian" captivity from which it could only be liberated by Christian Hellenism.

Gandillac, Maurice de (1906–2006). Professor of philosophy at the Sorbonne from 1946 to 1977 and a prolific writer on Nicolas of Cusa, Friedrich Nietzsche, and the origins of modernity. He was also the French translator of Dionysius the Areopagite. One of the most important of his books is *Genèses de la modernité* [Origins of Modernity] (Paris, 1992). He was on the jury that awarded Yannaras his Paris doctorate in 1970.

Gerontios, Elder. A hesychast monk and spiritual father of the Skete of Katounakia on Mount Athos.

Gilson, Étienne (1884–1978). Distinguished French historian of philosophy who made a major contribution to the twentieth-century revival of Thomism. From 1921 to 1932 he was professor of medieval history at the University of Paris. Later he taught at Harvard. During his time in North America, he founded the Pontifical Institute for Medieval Studies at Toronto. In 1946 he was elected a member of the Academie française. Vladimir Lossky studied under him for his doctorate on the Rhineland mystic Meister Eckhart.

Gregory I (ca. 540–604), St. Pope from 590 to 604 and a vigorous upholder of papal primacy who laid the foundations for the future papal state. In the East he is acknowledged as a saint on account of his *Dialogues* (important for the life of St Benedict), which at a very early date were translated into Greek.

Gregory VII (ca. 1020–1085). Pope from 1073 to his death, Gregory VII (originally Hildebrand) raised the mystique of the papacy to new heights with the twenty-seven propositions of *Dictatus papae*, which asserted papal authority over all secular rulers.

Gregory of Nyssa (ca. 330–ca. 395), St. The younger brother of St Basil the Great, Gregory is an outstanding theologian in the Origenian tradition influenced by Platonism. His exegetical and spiritual works have been particularly influential since Daniélou's work on him in the 1940s.

Hamakiotis, Athanasios (1891–1967). A hieromonk and charismatic priest of the Church of Panagia Neratziotissa at Maroussi, Athens. He founded a women's monastery dedicated to the Panagia Phaneromeni at Rodopolis in Attica.

Harnack, Adolph von (1851–1930). Lutheran church historian and professor successively at the universities of Giessen, Marburg, and Berlin. He was probably the most influential patristics scholar of his time, but attracted much opposition for holding that the early Christian gospel had been corrupted by the "Hellenization" of Christianity through the intrusion of Greek philosophy.

Hatzitheodorou, Theodoros. Professor of music at the Athens conservatoire (the Ōdeion Athēnōn). His students include well-known cantors such as Theodoros Vasilikos, the popularizer of Byzantine chant in the United States and Australia.

Heidegger, Martin (1889–1976). An important German philosopher of the twentieth century who has exercised an enormous influence on European philosophy. After early studies in theology, his philosophical interests were stimulated by Aristotle, who first posed the question about the nature of being, that is, about what it is that all existents have in common. He began teaching at the University of Freiburg in 1915. His most brilliant period was at the University of Marburg (1923–28), the period that saw the publication of his magnum opus, *Being and Time* (Oxford, 1962), originally published in German in 1927. Heidegger replaced the Cartesian thinking ego with *Dasein*, ("Being-there"), which has been described (by Michael Wheeler) as "the inherently social being who already operates with a pre-theoretical grasp of the a priori structures that make possible particular modes of being." The fundamental ontology that Heidegger proposed has informed all subsequent philosophical thought about the nature of being.

Helminiak, Daniel A. (1942–). Professor at the University of West Georgia, Carrollton, Georgia.

Henry, Gabriel (d. 1988). Orthodox priest in Paris. Fr Henry served the liturgy at the Russian church (Patriarchate of Moscow) of Sainte Geneviève (the patron of Paris), which had been founded in the rue de la Montagne-Sainte-Geneviève, near the saint's tomb and relics, by Fr Mikhail Belsky (who had had a dream of the saint) and members of the Brotherhood of St Photius. In 1966 the parish was transferred to the rue Saint-Victor in Paris's fifth arrondissement. In the last year of his life, Fr Henry was appointed rector of the Georgian Orthodox church of St Nino in the rue de la Rosière.

Ieronymos of Aegina (1883–1966). A Cappadocian who had known the ascetics in the cave churches of his homeland, Fr Ieronymos was deported to Greece upon the Greco-Turkish exchange of populations in 1924. He established himself on the island of Aegina, where he became a renowned elder much consulted for his spiritual discernment.

Isaac the Syrian (d. ca. 700), St. Monastic writer born in Qatar, who was made bishop of Nineveh (Mosul) by the Catholicos of the non-Ephesine Church of the East, and later retired to a life of desert solitude. Many of his homilies were translated into Greek and published in the eighteenth century. As a result, he has become an influential voice in monastic circles. Some of his homilies were included in the Russian *Philokalia*.

Jeremias II Tranos (1536–95). Ecumenical patriarch and a great pastor who did much to encourage the Orthodox communities under Ottoman rule and to strengthen monasticism on Mount Athos. He was approached by a group of Lutheran professors of Tübingen in 1573 to approve their Confession of Faith, but after examining it, he declined to do so. In 1589, however, while on a mission to Russia, he gave in to his hosts' pressure and raised the Metropolitanate of Moscow to patriarchal status.

Jerome (ca. 345–420), St. Born near Aquileia, at the head of the Adriatic, Jerome became an ascetic in Palestine and a great translator of Greek texts into Latin. The Latin version of the Bible, the Vulgate, is largely his work. A combative personality, he entered vigorously into a number of controversies, including those centered on Origen, Pelagius, and Jovinian.

Jevtić, Athanasios (1938–). Serbian bishop and patristics scholar. After graduating in theology from the University of Belgrade, Jevtić gained a doctorate in Athens on the ecclesiology of the Apostle Paul in St John Chrysostom (1968), and then studied at the Institute of St Sergius in Paris before returning to take up a post in the Faculty of Theology at the University of Belgrade. In 1991, at the end of his second term as dean of the faculty, he was made bishop of Banat. In the following year he became metropolitan of Bosnia and Herzegovina, at the beginning of NATO's intervention in the Bosnian war. Until his retirement in 1998, he proved an outstanding pastoral bishop at that time of great suffering for all of Bosnia's communities. In 2010, to the relief of the local Orthodox, he was invited to take over the administration of the Kosovo diocese, which had been split by feuding factions. His preaching and writing focusses on love as the foundation of knowledge.

John Chrysostom (ca. 347–407), St. Patriarch of Constantinople from 398, John was deposed by the Synod of the Oak in 403, returned briefly to his see, and then was deposed definitively in 407, when he died on his way into exile. His fiery sermons were popular with the general public for their denunciation of the sins of the rich and powerful, but he made enemies at court.

John of Sinai (ca. 570–ca. 649), St. An important witness to early hesychasm and the author of *The Ladder of Divine Ascent*, one of the great classics of monastic spiritual writing. He is also known as John Climacus.

Jovinian (d. ca. 405). A monk condemned by several Latin synods for holding that marriage was not an inferior state to consecrated virginity.

Kallistos (Ware) (1934–). Titular metropolitan of Diokleia and a widely read writer on Orthodoxy. Raised as an Anglican, Ware embraced Orthodoxy in 1958, at the age of twenty-four. In 1966 he was ordained a priest of the Ecumenical Patriarchate, and from 1966 to 2001 was Spalding lecturer in Eastern Orthodox Studies at the University of Oxford. In 1982 he became an auxiliary bishop of the metropolitan of Thyateira and Great Britain with the title Bishop of Diokleia. In 2007 the titular see of Diokleia was raised to a titular metropolitanate. Metropolitan Kallistos is a valued spiritual father and counselor. He has been well known to a broad public since the publication of his best-selling book *The Orthodox Church* (London, 1963) and its companion volume *The Orthodox Way* (London, 1979).

Kirill (Gundyaev) (1946–). Patriarch of Moscow and all Rus'. Born in Leningrad to a "Levitical" family (his father and grandfather were both priests), Vladimir (as he was baptized) Mikhailovich Gundyaev was tonsured and ordained a hieromonk with the name of Kirill in 1969. In 1976 he became bishop of Vyborg, and in 1984 archbishop of Smolensk and Vyazma, his title changing four years later to archbishop of Smolensk and Kaliningrad. He was elected patriarch in 2009. Shortly after his enthronement he spoke of the Byzantine concept of *symphonia* as summarizing the ideal relationship that ought to exist between Church and state.

Korais, Adamantios (1748–1833). Man of the Enlightenment and guiding spirit of the Greek state that was established in the southern tip of the Balkans after the War of Independence (1821–1829) from the Ottoman Empire. Born in in Smyrna on the Aegean coast of Asia Minor, Korais was educated at the famous Evangelical School of that city. He then studied medicine in France at the University of Montpellier (1782–1787) before going to Paris, where he lived for the rest of his life. In Paris he experienced the French Revolution of 1789, whose ideals he embraced. A critic of the clergy and of the Ecumenical Patriarchate, which he saw as a tool of the Ottoman authorities, he promoted his ideas chiefly through the publication of classical texts with long introductions. His disciples were able to implement his ideas on the classicising reform of the Greek language and the creation of a state church on a Protestant model in the Hellenic kingdom established in 1833.

Koutroubis, Dimitrios (1921–83). A remarkable thinker who never held any academic or ecclesiastical office yet made a vital contribution to the Greek theological renaissance of the 1960s. Impressed by the theological culture of some Jesuits he met in Athens during the Second World War, Koutroubis became a Roman Catholic and pursued studies in philosophy and theology at Jesuit centers in England and France. He left the Jesuits before ordination and in 1954 returned to Orthodoxy. His house at Vouliagmeni, near Athens, where he lived a largely hidden life, became an "oasis" where people could go to talk and learn about the Greek Fathers. The contributions to "In Memoriam Demetrios Koutroubis"

(*Sobornost* 6.1 [1984]: 67–77) include a brief essay by Christos Yannaras.

Küng, Hans (1928–). Modernist Swiss Catholic theologian and powerful critic of the Vatican. Ordained in 1954, Küng became a professor of theology at the University of Tübingen in 1960. Two years later, at the opening of the Second Vatican Council, he was invited to Rome by Pope John XXIII as a *peritus* (theological expert). Subsequently he expressed his opposition to the doctrine of papal infallibility, and in 1979 he was deprived of his licence to teach as a Catholic theologian. He was obliged to resign from Tübingen's Catholic faculty but remained at the university until his retirement in 1996 as a professor of ecumenical theology.

Kyprianos (Koutsoumbas) (1935–2013). Kyprianos became Old Calendarist bishop of Oropos and Fili but was deposed by the Old Calendarist synod in 1986 for "the heresy of ecumenism" (i.e., for holding the view that the grace of the Holy Spirit was still operative in the Church of Greece, which—along with Romania—had accepted the Gregorian Calendar in 1924). Kyprianos did not accept his deposition; he founded his own Synod-in-Resistance.

Lacan, Jacques (1901–81). French psychologist who reread Freud in the light of modern philosophy and linguistics. His annual seminars (from 1953 to 1981) at the University of Paris attracted a strong interdisciplinary following.

Le Goff, Jacques (1924–2014). French medieval historian of the *Annales* school who succeeded Fernand Braudel in 1972 as head of the École des hautes études en sciences sociales in Paris. Two of his influential books translated into English are *The Medieval Imagination* (Chicago, 1988) and *The Birth of Europe* (Oxford, 2005).

Lévinas, Emmanuel (1906–95). Distinguished French philosopher and public intellectual who taught that all ethics derive from confrontation with the Other. Born to a Jewish family in Lithuania, Lévinas came to France after the Russian Revolution and studied philosophy at the University of Strasbourg. His doctoral thesis of 1930 was on the phenomenology of Husserl, under whom he had studied at Freiburg. Most of his teaching career was spent as a professor of philosophy at the Sorbonne in Paris. His most influential book in English is *Totality and Infinity* (Pittsburgh, 1969).

Lopez, Robert S. (1910–86). American medieval historian of the Mediterranean world. Born in Genoa, Lopez came to the United States shortly before the Second Word War. In 1946 he began a thirty-five year career with Yale University, which saw him become the Sterling professor of history. His best-known book is *The Commercial Revolution of the Middle Ages* (Prentice-Hall, 1971).

Lorentzatos, Zissimos (1915–2004). Greek literary critic and poet (he was the translator of Eliot's *The Waste Land*) who reflected deeply on the spiritual tradition of the Orthodox Church, not as an exclusive national possession, but as a resource enabling the Greeks to become "a holy people for Christ." Collections of his essays available in English include *The Lost Center and Other Essays in Greek Poetry* (Princeton, NJ, 1980), *Drama of Quality (Romiosyne)* (Limni, Greece, 1996), and *Aegean Notebooks* (Limni, Greece, 2013).

Lossky, Nicholas. Archpriest Nicolas Lossky, son of Vladimir Lossky, is a professor emeritus of the University of Paris X–Nanterre, where he taught a course in British civilization, and also professor of the history of the Church in the West at the Institute of St Sergius. He is the author of a notable book on the English seventeenth-century divine Lancelot Andrewes (Oxford, 1991).

Lossky, Vladimir (1903–58). One of the most important Orthodox theologians of the twentieth century. Exiled from Russia in 1922 with his father Nikolai, who was professor of philosophy at the University of St Petersburg, Lossky came to Paris, where he pursued studies in medieval philosophy at the Sorbonne. For much of his life, he taught dogmatic theology and Church history at the Theological Institute of St Denis in Paris. His work of 1944 on the apophatic character of mystical theology, published in English as *The Mystical Theology of the Eastern Church* (London, 1957), rapidly became a classic.

Louth, Andrew (1944–). Orthodox priest and professor emeritus of patristic and Byzantine studies at the University of Durham. Fr Louth, a former Anglican, is a distinguished patristics scholar and theologian. His most recent book is *Modern Orthodox Thinkers* (London, 2015).

Lubac, Henri de (1896–1991). Jesuit theologian who was a central figure in the movement of *la nouvelle théologie*, as its critics dubbed it, which sought to exploit the resources of the Greek Fathers in opposition to the neoscholasticism that dominated Catholic theology before the Second Vatican Council. He was made a cardinal in 1983.

Makris, Amphilochios (1889–1970). Elder of the Monastery of St John the Theologian on Patmos and a much-loved spiritual father. He entered the monastery in 1906, was tonsured to the great schema in 1913, and was ordained to the priesthood in 1919. In 1935 he was elected abbot, but in 1937 he was exiled by the Italians (who governed the Dodecanese at that time) for his apostolic activities, which included the foundation of a women's monastery. On his return in 1939, he did not resume his office, but devoted himself to a life of spiritual fatherhood.

Mark Eugenikos (ca. 1394–1445), St. Metropolitan of Ephesus from 1437 to 1445. He was the leading speaker on the Greek side, along with Bessarion, at the Council of Florence (1438–39) and the only member of the Greek delegation who refused to sign the Decree of Union. In his theological works he takes a strong Palamite position.

Maximus the Confessor (ca. 580–662), St. Perhaps of Palestinian origin, Maximus became a monk in about 614. His vision of cosmic history as a process leading to the deification of man in Christ made him one of the greatest of patristic theologians. His defense of orthodox Christology against monotheletism (which denied both a human and a divine will in Christ) led to his trial for heresy in Constantinople and to his death in exile shortly afterward.

Metz, Johann Baptist (1928–). Influential German Catholic theologian. Metz is professor emeritus of fundamental theology at the University of Münster. He studied the thought of Heidegger and Aquinas under Karl Rahner but turned away from the latter's transcendental theology in favor of a theology rooted in Christian *praxis*. He is a strong critic of Christianity in the form of a "bourgeois religion."

Meyendorff, John (1926–92). Outstanding Orthodox Church historian and theologian, particularly noted for his groundbreaking work on St Gregory Palamas. Meyendorff was born in Paris to émigré parents of the Russian nobility. He studied at the St Sergius Theological Institute and also at the Sorbonne, where he obtained his doctorate in 1958 for his work on Palamas, published as *Introduction à l'étude de Grégoire Palamas* (Paris, 1959) (abbreviated English translation: *A Study of Gregory Palamas* [Leighton Buzzard, 1964]). In 1959 he was ordained and moved to New York, where he was appointed professor of Church history and patristics at St Vladimir's Orthodox Seminary. In 1967 he also became professor of Byzantine history at Fordham University, and from 1984 to 1992 he was dean of St Vladimir's.

Nellas, Panayiotis (1936–86). An important figure in the Greek theological renaissance of the 1960s, who wrote extensively on Nicholas Kabasilas and was the founder of the journal *Synaxē*. His influential work *Zōon theoumenon* has been translated into English as *Deification in Christ: The Nature of the Human Person* (Crestwood, NY, 1987).

Nikodemos the Haghiorite (1749–1809), St. One of the leaders of the Kollyvades movement, an eighteenth-century movement of spiritual and ecclesial renewal, who published several spiritual works (including *Unseen Warfare* [1776] and *A Handbook of Spiritual Counsel* [1801], both available in English translation) based on the Greek translations of Italian Roman Catholic originals. With St Makarios of Corinth, he also compiled and published the *Philokalia* (Venice, 1782). Nikodemos was glorified as a saint by the Ecumenical Patriarchate in 1955.

Ouspensky, Leonid (1902–1987). Iconographer and lay theologian. Ouspensky's path from revolutionary Russia to Paris was unusual. Having become an atheist in his teens, he joined the Red Army and fought on the Bolshevik side in the Civil War. Taken prisoner by the Whites, he was evacuated with them from South Russia. On arrival in France, he worked in factory jobs before enrolling in an art school in Paris. It was his attempt there to paint an icon that brought him back to Orthodoxy. He joined the Brotherhood of St Photius (through which he became a friend of Lossky's) and in 1944 began a forty-year career teaching courses of icon paining at the Theological Institute of St Denis. His book on icons, coauthored with Vladimir Lossky, *The Meaning of Icons* (Crestwood, NY, 1982), remains valuable.

Paisios of Mount Athos (1924–94), St. Born in Pharasa of Cappadocia, he was baptized Arsenios by St Arsenios of Cappadocia, who predicted a monastic future for him. Shortly afterward, he came to Greece as a result of the 1924 Greco-Turkish exchange of populations. He was tonsured on Mount Athos in 1954 with the name of Paisios (after an archbishop of Caesarea who originated from Pharasa) and lived at a variety of hermitages on Athos until 1993, when an operation for cancer prevented him from returning to his beloved Holy Mountain. He then went to live at St John the Theologian at Souroti, a women's monastery he had helped to found just outside Thessalonica. As he was by now a renowned spiritual father, queues of people waited to see him each day for his counsel and blessing. He was glorified by the Holy Synod of the Ecumenical Patriarchate in 2015, with his feast day on July 12.

Palamas, Gregory (ca. 1296–1359), St. Great defender of the hesychasts' path to communion with God and ultimate deification. The distinction he made between the essence and the energies of God was examined by four successive Constantinopolitan church councils from 1341 to 1368 and on each occasion was vindicated. In the early twentieth century, his teaching again became a matter of controversy between his neo-Thomist detractors and his Orthodox defenders. John Meyendorff made an outstanding contribution to Palamas studies with his monograph *Introduction à l'étude de Grégoire Palamas* and his critical text of Palamas' *Triads*, both published in 1959.

Papadiamantis, Alexandros (1851–1911). Greek novelist and short-story writer and a seminal figure in modern Greek literature. The son of a priest, he spent his life among the poor in Athens and on his native island of Skiathos. Living very simply as he did by writing and translating and never marrying, he gained the reputation of a *kosmokalogeros*, a monk-in-the-world. His deep Christian faith permeates his writing, although very few of his works are on specifically religious themes. Most of his work has been published in English translation.

Papanikolaou, Aristotle. Professor of Orthodox theology and culture at Fordham University, New York, and codirector, with George Demacopoulos, of the Orthodox Christian Studies Center at the same university. He is the author of a study that engages particularly with the thinking of Lossky and Zizioulas: *Being with God* (Notre Dame, 2006).

Papanoutsos, Evangelos (1900–1982). Major Greek writer on philosophical, historical, and cultural themes. After studies in Athens and Alexandria, he gained his doctorate at Tübingen in 1927 with a dissertation on religious experience in Plato. He taught at several Greek academies during his career, and from 1946 to 1967 wrote a column for the newspaper *To Bēma*.

Pascal, Blaise (1623–62). French mathematician, philosopher, and spiritual writer. His most widely read work is his posthumously published *Pensées*, reflections on faith and reason, soul and matter, life and death, and similar themes.

Paul (Tsaousoglou), Metropolitan of Glyphada (1943–). First metropolitan of Glyfada, a new diocese in the suburbs of Athens carved out of the diocese of Nea Smyrni in 2002.

Payne, Daniel P. Assistant priest at Annunciation Greek Orthodox Cathedral in Houston, Texas, and an independent scholar.

Petrà, Basilio (1946–). Professor of moral theology at the Faculty of Theology of Central Italy (Florence). Fr Petrà, who is of Greek descent, is the translator of several of Yannaras's books into Italian.

Philaret (Drozdov) (1782–1867), St. Metropolitan of Moscow from 1821 to 1867. Philaret's published sermons were widely read, and his *Christian Catechism* (1833) established itself as the standard theological manual in Russia for the whole of the nineteenth century.

Pikionis, Dimitrios (1887–1968). Distinguished Greek architect known for his buildings that are modernist yet at the same time perfectly rooted in the Greek spiritual tradition. After studies in Athens, Paris, and Munich, he worked mainly in Athens, where he created the landscaped paths on the Acropolis and on the adjacent Filopappou Hill, together with the little church there of Agios Dimitrios Loumbardiaris.

Platon (Levshin) (1737–1812). Archbishop and then metropolitan of Moscow from 1775 to 1812. A gifted orator, Platon's preaching brought him to the attention of the Empress Catherine. He became tutor to the tsarevich, for whom he wrote a catechism colored by the Enlightenment ideas dominant at the time. As metropolitan of Moscow, Platon was conciliatory toward the Old Believers and other dissenters.

Porphyrios (Bairaktaris) (1906–91), St. Renowned elder and spiritual father. Born on the island of Euboia, Porphyrios became a monk on Mount Athos in his early teens at the Skete of Kafsokalyvia. On his return to his home village to recover after an illness, he was unexpectedly ordained. From 1940 to 1970 he was a hospital chaplain in Athens. In 1984 he returned to Athos to the same cell that he had originally occupied. His sanctity was officially recognized by the Holy Synod of the Ecumenical Patriarchate in 2013 (feast day December 2).

Rahner, Karl (1904–84). Jesuit theologian and outstanding philosophical thinker. A prolific author, his main achievement was perhaps to revamp contemporary Thomism with the help of Heidegger's metaphysical insights.

Ramsey, Michael (1904–88). Archbishop of Canterbury from 1961 to 1974. Ramsey was a theologian whose deep knowledge of the Fathers created in him a profound sympathy for Orthodoxy. Among his publications, *The Gospel and the Catholic Church* (London, 1936) and *The Glory of God and the Transfiguration of Christ* (London, 1949) remain especially valuable.

Ratzinger, Josef (1927–), Pope Benedict XVI emeritus. After teaching in several German universities, Ratzinger became archbishop of Munich in 1977, prefect of the Congregation of the Doctrine of the Faith in 1981, and pope in 2005. He resigned in 2013, due to infirmities of advanced age. In 1969 he was, with von Balthasar, de Lubac, and others, one of the cofounders of *Communio*. As cardinal and pope, he opposed relativism and secularism in the Church and was a strong defender of traditional Catholic doctrine.

Romanides, John (1927–2001). Brilliant, if controversial, Greek-American theologian. Romanides studied at Holy Cross in Boston and at the University of Athens, where he defended an outstanding doctoral thesis on original sin (English translation: *The Ancestral Sin* [Glen Rock, NJ, 2002]). As a result of his passionate advocacy of *Rōmēosynē* ("Roman Greekness"), his hostility to Augustine, and his strong attachment to Palamite hesychasm, Romanides is regarded as one of the most anti-Western of Orthodox theologians.

Sartre, Jean-Paul (1905–80). French existentialist philosopher whose literary works and left-wing political activism made him one of the best-known philosophers of the twentieth century. His magnum opus, *Being and Nothingness* (1943), continues to be important for its insights into the human agent as presence-to-itself.

Saward, John (1947–). Fellow of Greyfriars, Oxford, and formerly professor of dogmatic theology at the International Theological Institute, Gaming, Austria. Saward's first book, *Perfect Fools: Folly for Christ's Sake in Catholic and Orthodox Spirituality* (Oxford, 1980), reflected an early interest in Orthodoxy, but his subsequent publications have focused purely on modern Roman Catholic theology. Originally an Anglican, he was received into the Roman Catholic Church in 1979 and ordained to the priesthood (as a married man) in 2003.

Schillebeeckx, Edward (1914–2009). Belgian Dominican theologian. Schillebeeckx was highly influential at the Second Vatican Council, not as an official *peritus*, but as a trusted adviser of the Dutch bishops. Because he was in favor of episcopal collegiality and hostile to the doctrine of papal infallibility, his orthodoxy was investigated several times by the Vatican. He taught for most of his career at the Catholic University of Nijmegen in the Netherlands.

Schmemann, Alexander (1921–83). Eminent theologian of the Russian diaspora. Schmemann taught Church history at the St Sergius Theological Institute in Paris for five years (1946–1951) before being invited to join St Vladimir's Orthodox Seminary in New York. He was dean of St Vladimir's from 1962 until his death. In 1970 he participated in the foundation of the Orthodox Church in America (OCA) as an autocephalous offshoot of the Russian Orthodox Church. He broadcast in Russian to the Soviet Union for thirty years, numbering among his many appreciative listeners Alexander Solzhenitsyn. *The Journals of Father Alexander Schmemann*, covering the last decade of his life, were published posthumously by St Vladimir's Seminary Press (Crestwood, NY, 2000).

Seferis, George (1900–71). Born in Smyrna, the son of a lawyer, Seferis studied law and literature in Paris before entering the Greek diplomatic service in 1926. His work as a poet and translator (especially of Eliot) marks a new era in Greek poetry after the age of Cavafy. In 1962 he was awarded the Nobel Prize for literature.

Sherrard, Philip (1922–1995). A translator of modern Greek poetry and remarkable lay theologian whom Metropolitan Kallistos has called "a creative and sometimes prophetic interpreter of the living tradition of the Orthodox Church." His last work, which collects many of his writings, was published posthumously as *Christianity: Lineaments of a Sacred Tradition* (Boston, 1998).

Silouan the Athonite (1866–1938), St. Russian ascetic of Mount Athos. Silouan entered the Russian monastery of St Panteleimon in 1892 and lived a hidden life of hesychastic prayer there until his death. He has become widely known through the book of his disciple, Archimandrite Sophrony, *Saint Silouan the Athonite* (Crestwood, NY, 1999), first published in London in 1952 as *The Undistorted Image*. He was placed in the canon of saints by the Ecumenical Patriarchate in 1987.

Siricius (ca. 334–99), St. Bishop of Rome from 384 to his death. He was a vigorous pope who fought to prevent East Illyria (modern Serbia) from being removed from his jurisdiction and attached to Constantinople. It was in 392 that he condemned Jovinian.

Stephen Dušan (1308–55). King of Serbia and self-styled emperor of the Serbs, Greeks, and Albanians (1346–55) who sought to bring all Byzantine territories in Macedonia and Thrace under his rule. He promoted the Serbian Church from an archbishopric to a patriarchate centered on Peć.

Struve, Pierre (1924–68). Grandson of the Russian economist and statesman P. B. Struve (1870–1944), Pierre Struve was ordained a priest in 1964 and served in the crypt church of the Russian Cathedral in Paris on the rue Daru while continuing to practice as a doctor. He was in favor of an Orthodoxy open to French culture, and became widely known for his monthly television program *Orthodoxie*.

Symeon (864/5–927). Ruler of Bulgaria from 893 to 927 and founder of the First Bulgarian Empire, which extended from the Adriatic to the Black Sea. He raised the Bulgarian Church to a patriarchate, with the patriarch's seat at Symeon's capital, Preslav.

Theodoulos, Elder (d. 1966). Spiritual father and founder, in 1918, of the women's monastery of St John the Baptist at Koroni, on the south coast of Greece. He gave instruction regularly at a "school" he established just below the monastery.

Theokletos Dionysiatis (1916–2006). Learned Athonite elder and author noted for his rigorist outlook. Fr Theokletos entered the monastery of Dionysiou on Mount Athos in 1941 and served his noviciate under the saintly elder (later abbot) Fr Gabriel. His first book, *Between Heaven and Earth*, on the monastic life, was awarded a prize by the Academy of Athens. Among his many works are monographs on St Gregory Palamas, St Nikodemos the Hagiorite, and Alexandros Papadiamantis.

Theokritoff, Elizabeth. Independent scholar well known for her presentation of an Orthodox approach to ecological issues in *Living in God's Creation* (Crestwood, NY, 2006). Under her maiden name (Briere), she was the translator of Yannaras's first book to appear in English (*The Freedom of Morality* [Crestwood, NY, 1984]).

Thomas Aquinas (1225–74). The greatest philosopher of the Middle Ages, Thomas joined the Dominican order at a critical time when the full corpus of Aristotle's writings first became available in the West. His distinctions between philosophy and theology, faith and reason, essence and existence, remain fundmental for Western thought.

Tracy, David (1939–). American Roman Catholic theologian who spent most of his teaching career at the University of Chicago

Divinity School. His main contribution to theological thought has been in hermeneutics and theological method.

Trembelas, Panayiotis (1886–1977). Professor of practical theology at the University of Athens from 1939 to 1957 and leading member of the Zoe movement from 1911 to 1956, when he left to found a similar brotherhood called Sōtēr. His best-known work is his three-volume *Dogmatics*, of which a French translation was published by the Monastery of Chevetogne in 1966–68.

Vasileios (Gontikakis) (1936–). One of the group of important Greek theologians who transformed theological thinking in the 1960s. In Fr Vasileios's case, he was tonsured as a monk on Mount Athos, where he made a significant contribution to the revival of monastic life. Currently abbot of Iveron, he is best known for his book *Eisodikon*, translated into English as *Hymn of Entry* (Crestwood, NY, 1984).

Vassiliadis, Petros (1945–). Biblical scholar and professor emeritus of the University of Thessalonica. A disciple of Agouridis, he has sought to emphasize the biblical foundation of Orthodox theology. He has also played a significant role in the World Council of Churches.

Vlachos, Hierotheos (1945–). Metropolitan of Nafpaktos and Agios Vlasios in Greece since 1995. A student of hesychasm and a disciple of Fr John Romanides (1921–2007), Metropolitan Hierotheos is the author of several books teaching a therapeutic view of salvation.

Wallace-Hadrill, J. M. (1916–1985). Leading historian of the Merovingian period of European history. Wallace-Hadrill was Chichele professor of modern history in the University of Oxford from 1974 to 1984, and a fellow of All Souls College from 1974 until his death.

Williams, Rowan (1950–). Distinguished Anglican theologian and former archbishop of Canterbury. Williams has always had a profound interest in Orthodoxy. His essay on Yannaras's theology of personhood, published in *Sobornost* in 1972, was the first serious study of Yannaras's thought in English and has remained important. His 1975 Oxford doctorate (supervised by A. M. Allchin) was on the theology of Vladimir Lossky. Williams's Orthodox interest has been maintained, as his 2008 study of Dostoevsky shows (*Dostoevsky: Language, Faith and Fiction* [London, 2008]). Since 2013 he has been master of Magdalene College, Cambridge.

Wittgenstein, Ludwig (1889–1951). One of the defining philosophers of the twentieth century. Born in Vienna to a rich family of Jewish decent, Wittgenstein went to Cambridge, England, in 1911 to study philosophy with Bertrand Russell. The slim volume that he published in 1921, *Tractatus Logico-Positivus*, which investigates the relationship between logical propositions and the world, marked a turning point in twentieth-century philosophy. From 1929 to 1947 he taught at Cambridge, but he published hardly anything else in his lifetime. His posthumous *Philosophical Investigations* (Oxford, 1953) reveal a move toward the determination of meaning from the usage of words in what he called a "language-game," the particular context in which a word is used.

Zambelios, Spyridon (1815–81). Greek historian who in the nineteenth century constructed one of the principal narratives of neo-Hellenic identity. Reacting against the habit of Western scholars (and their Greek imitators) of jumping straight from antiquity to modern times, he maintained that Byzantium was the vital link between classical antiquity and the neo-Hellenes. The element of continuity was provided by the Orthodox Church and its dogmatic formulations, which, along with the popular linguistic tradition, saved Greek identity from irretrievable Westernization. His chief publications are a collection of demotic songs (1852) and a volume of Byzantine studies (1857).

Zenkovsky, Vasilii (1881–1962). Distinguished Russian émigré philosopher. At the outbreak of the Russian Revolution, Zenkovsky was a professor at the University of Kiev. He became minister of religion in Kerensky's provisional government but was forced to leave Russia during the civil war. In 1927 he came to Paris, where he was appointed to teach philosophy at the Theological Institute of St Sergius. He was ordained to the priesthood in 1944, subsequently becoming dean of St Sergius. His two-volume *Histoire de la philosophie russe* (Paris, 1953–54) is still in print.

Zervakos, Philotheos (1884–1980). An elder much revered in Greece. Fr Philotheos became a monk in 1902 and was ordained to the priesthood ten years later. At the monastery of Longovarda on the Aegean island of Paros, where he became abbot in 1930, he exercised a ministry of spiritual fatherhood for nearly seventy years. There is a life of him by Constantine Cavarnos, *Blessed Elder Philotheos Zervakos* (Belmont, MA, 1993).

Zizioulas, John (1931–). Greek theologian with an international reputation for his work on eucharistic ecclesiology and the theology of the person. After graduating from the Universities of Thessaloniki and Athens, Zizioulas carried out doctoral research at Harvard under Florovsky, and he returned to Greece to gain a doctorate at the University of Athens in 1965. He then taught at the Universities of Edinburgh, Glasgow, and London (where a personal chair in systematic theology was created for him) until 1986, when he was elected, while still a layman, to become a titular metropolitan (of Pergamon) of the Holy Synod of the Ecumenical Patriarchate. His most influential works in English are *Being as Communion* (Crestwood, NY, 1985) and *Communion and Otherness* (London, 2006).

Bibliography

Works of Christos Yannaras in English Translation

"Orthodoxy and the West." Translated by Theodore Stylianopoulos. *Eastern Churches Review* 3.3 (1971): 286–300.

"Theology in Present-Day Greece." Translated by Angeline Bouchard. *St Vladimir's Theological Quarterly* 16 (1972): 195–214.

"The Distinction between Essence and Energies and Its Importance for Theology." *St Vladimir's Theological Quarterly* 19 (1975): 232–45.

"A Note on Political Theology." Translated by Steven Peter Tsichlis. *St Vladimir's Theological Quarterly* 27.1 (1983): 53–56. Reprinted in Fr Gregory Edwards and Herman A. Middleton, eds., *The Meaning of Reality: Essays on Existence and Communion, Eros and History*, 149–52 (Los Angeles and Athens: Sebastian Press and Indiktos, 2011).

The Freedom of Morality. Translated by Elizabeth Briere. Crestwood, NY: St Vladimir's Seminary Press, 1984.

Elements of Faith: An Introduction to Orthodox Theology. Translated by Keith Schram. Edinburgh: T&T Clark, 1991.

"The Church in the Postcommunist World." *International Journal for the Study of the Christian Church* 3.1 (2003): 29–46. A different version, under the title "The Church in Post-Communist Europe," was published as a separate booklet in the same year by InterOrthodox Press of Berkeley, California, and was reprinted in Edwards and Middleton, eds., *The Meaning of Reality*, 123–43.

"Human Rights and the Orthodox Church." In *The Orthodox Churches in a Pluralistic World: An Ecumenical Conversation*, edited by E. Clapsis, 83–89. Brookline, MA: Holy Cross Orthodox Press, 2004. Reprinted in Edwards and Middleton, eds., *The Meaning of Reality*, 43–50.

Postmodern Metaphysics. Translated by Norman Russell. Brookline, MA: Holy Cross Orthodox Press, 2004.

On the Absence and Unknowability of God: Heidegger and the Areopagite. Edited with an introduction by Andrew Louth. Translated by Haralambos Ventis. London and New York: T&T Clark International, 2005.

Variations on the Song of Songs. Translated by Norman Russell. Brookline, MA: Holy Cross Orthodox Press, 2005.

Orthodoxy and the West: Hellenic Self-Identity in the Modern Age. Translated by Peter Chamberas and Norman Russell. Brookline, MA: Holy Cross Orthodox Press, 2006.

Person and Eros. Translated by Norman Russell. Brookline, MA: Holy Cross Orthodox Press, 2007.

"Proposal for a New Ecclesiastical Service of Marriage." Translated with an introduction by Andrew Louth as "A revised Orthodox ceremony of marriage?" *Sobornost* 29.2 (2007): 51–74. Reprinted in Edwards and Middleton, eds., *The Meaning of Reality*, 93–113.

The Meaning of Reality: Essays on Existence and Communion, Eros and History. Edited by Fr Gregory Edwards and Herman A. Middleton. Los Angeles and Athens: Sebastian Press & Indiktos, 2011.

Relational Ontology. Translated by Norman Russell. Brookline, MA: Holy Cross Orthodox Press, 2011.

The Enigma of Evil. Translated by Norman Russell. Brookline, MA: Holy Cross Orthodox Press, 2012.

Against Religion: The Alienation of the Ecclesial Event. Translated by Norman Russell. Brookline, MA: Holy Cross Orthodox Press, 2013.

The Schism in Philosophy: The Hellenic Perspective and Its Western Reversal. Translated by Norman Russell. Brookline, MA: Holy Cross Orthodox Press, 2015.

Selected Studies on Christos Yannaras

Angelis, Dimitris et al. *Chrēstos Giannaras* [Christos Yannaras]. Athens: Manifesto, 2015.

Cole, Jonathan, "Personhood in the digital age: the ethical use of new information technologies." *St Mark's Review* 233 (2015): 60–73.

Grigoropoulou, Evaggelia. "The Early Development of the Thought of Christos Yannaras." D.Phil. thesis, University of Durham, Department of Theology and Religion, 2008.

Kalaitzidis, P., A. N. Papathanasiou, and Th. Ampatzidis, eds. *Anataraxeis stē metapolemikē theologia. Hē "Theologia tou '60"* [The shake-up in postwar theology: The "theology of the '60s"]. Athens: Indiktos, 2009.

Louth, Andrew. Introduction to Christos Yannaras, *On the Absence and Unknowability of God*, 1–14. London and New York: T&T Clark International, 2005.

_____. "Some Recent Works by Christos Yannaras in English Translation." *Modern Theology* 25.2 (2009): 329–40.

_____. "Lay Theologians: Dimitris Koutroubis, Christos Yannaras, Stelios Ramfos." In idem, *Modern Orthodox Thinkers: From the Philokalia to the Present*, 247–63. London: SPCK, 2015.

Mitralexis, Sotiris. "Person, Eros, Critical Ontology: An Attempt to Recapitulate Christos Yannaras' Philosophy." *Sobornost* 34.1 (2012): 33–40.

Nichols, Adrian. "Christos Yannaras and Theological Ethics." In idem, *Light from the East: Authors and Themes in Orthodox Theology*, 181–93. London: Sheed & Ward, 1995.

Nissiotis, Nikos. "Orthodoxy and the West: A Response." *The Greek Orthodox Theological Review* 17 (1972): 132–42.

Panagiotopoulos, I. "Re-Appraising the Subject and the Social in Western Philosophy and in Contemporary Orthodox Thought." *Studies in East European Thought* 58.4 (2006): 299–330.

Papanikolaou, Aristotle. "Orthodoxy, Post-Modernism, and Ecumenism: The Difference that Divine-Human Communion Makes." *Journal of Ecumenical Studies* 42.4 (2007): 527–46.

_____. "Personhood and its Exponents in Twentieth-Century Orthodox Theology." In *The Cambridge Companion to Orthodox Christian Theology*, edited by Mary B. Cunningham and Elizabeth Theokritoff, 232–45. Cambridge: Cambridge University Press, 2008.

_____. *The Mystical as Political: Democracy and Non-Radical Ortho-doxy.* Notre Dame, IN: University of Notre Dame Press, 2012.

Payne. Daniel P. "An Eastern Orthodox Critique of Rawlsian Liberalism: The Personal Ontology of Christos Yannaras." *LiveJournal. com.* July 27, 2006. *http://sbulgakov.livejournal.com/43546.html.*

_____. "Orthodoxy, Islam and the 'Problem' of the West: a Comparison of the Liberation Theologies of Christos Yannaras and Sayyid Qutb." *Religion, State and Society* 36.4 (2008): 435–50.

_____. *The Revival of Political Hesychasm in Contemporary Orthodox Thought: The Political Hesyhasm of John S. Romanides and Christos Yannaras.* Lanham, MD: Lexington Books, 2011.

_____. "The 'Relational Ontology' of Christos Yannaras: The Hesychastic Influence on the Understanding of the Person in the Thought of Christos Yannaras." *https://www.academia.edu/1479462.*

Petrà, Basilio. "Personalist Thought in Greece in the Twentieth Century: A First Tentative Synthesis." *The Greek Orthodox Theological Review* 50 (2005): 2–48.

_____. "Christos Yannaras and the Idea of 'Dysis.'" In *Orthodox Constructions of the West*, edited by George E. Demacopoulos and Aristotle Papanikolaou, 161–80. New York: Fordham University Press, 2013.

_____. *Christos Yannaras.* Brescia, Italy: Morcelliana, 2015.

Prevelakis, Nicolas. "Theologies as Alternative Histories: John Romanides and Christos Yannaras." In *Classic@Online Journal* 10 (2014). Republished at Center for Hellenic Studies, Harvard University. http://chs.harvard.edu/CHS/article/display/4889.

Ramfos, Stelios. *Yearning for the One: Chapters in the Inner Life of the Greeks.* Translated by Norman Russell. Brookline, MA: Holy Cross Orthodox Press, 2011.

Russell, Norman. "Modern Greek Theologians and the Greek Fathers," *Philosophy and Theology* 18.1 (2006): 77–92.

_____. "Christos Yannaras (1935–) and Panayiotis Nellas (1936–1986)—Transcending Created Finitude." In *Creation and Salvation*, vol. 2, *A Companion on Recent Theological Movements*, edited by Ernst M. Conradie, 51–55. Berlin: LIT Verlag, 2012.

_____. "Christos Yannaras." In *Key Theological Thinkers: From Modern to Postmodern*, edited by Staale Johannes Kristiansen and Sven Rise, 725–34. Farnham, UK: Ashgate, 2013.

_____. "The enduring significance of Christos Yannaras: Some further works in translation." *International Journal for the Study of the Christian Church* 16.1 (2016): 58–65.

Stoeckl, K. *Community after Totalitariansm: The Russian Orthodox Intellectual Tradition and the Philosophical Discourse of Modernity*. Frankfurt: Peter Lang, 2008.

_____. "Contemporary Orthodox Discourses on Human Rights: The Standpoint of Christos Yannaras in a Political Philosophical Perspective." In *Orthodox Christianity and Human Rights*, edited by Evert van der Zweerde and Alfons Brüning, 185–99. Louvaine, Belgium: Peeters, 2012.

Sumares, Manuel. "Signifying the Mystical as Struggle: Yannaras' Orthodox Refiguring of Philosophy of Language." *Annals of the University of Bucharest, Philosophy Series* 63.1 (2014): 3–15.

Swinburne, Richard. "A Response to Christos Yannaras' *Against Religion*." *Oxbridge Philokalic Review* 2 (2013): 54–60.

Ware, Kallistos. "Scholasticism and Orthodoxy: Theological Method as a Factor in the Schism." *Eastern Churches Review* 5.1 (1973): 16–27.

Williams, R. D. "The Theology of Personhood: A Study of the Thought of Christos Yannaras." *Sobornost* 6, 1st series (1972): 415–30.

Index

Bulgaria, 125, 163
Byzantium, 81, 91, 118

catholicity, 126
Causal Principle, 41–2, 71–2, 98,
   100–1, 115
Cavafy, C. P., 37, 173
celibacy, 110–13, 131, 155
Chalcedon, Council of, 133
Charlemagne, 64
Chenu, Marie-Dominique, 12, 65,
   83, 103, 135, 173
China, 158
Chitty, Derwas, 64, 173
Christ, Jesus. See Jesus Christ; Logos
Christianity, 81, 91. See also Church;
   faith/trust; Orthodox Church;
   Roman Catholic Church
Christification, 78
Church, 21, 40, 67–8, 72–3, 79, 80–
   1, 83, 102–3, 108, 110, 115–16,
   123, 124–5, 135, 151–3, 154.
   See also ecclesia; ecclesiology;
   Orthodox Church; Orthodoxism;
   Roman Catholic Church
Cistercians, 64
Clément, Olivier, 38, 39, 173–4
Cluny, 64
Cole, Jonathan, 26
collegiality. See synod
communion, 58, 61
communism, 53
Concilium (journal), 65
Congar, Yves, 65, 153, 155, 174
Constantinople, patriarchate of. See
   Patriarchate, Ecumenical
consumerism, 25
council. See synod

createdness, 70; mode of, 107, 109,
   135
Crete, University of, 14
Crusade, Fourth (1204), 133

Danielaioi of Katounakia, 36
Daniélou, Jean, 64, 153, 155, 174
Daru, rue, Paris, 38
Davies, Oliver, 31
death, 17, 18, 50, 65, 99, 115; "of
   God," 44
deification. See theōsis
democracy, 90–1
deontology, 39
Depraz, N., 26
Descartes, René, 53, 64, 174
desire (epithymia), 108–9
dialogue, ecumenical, 115–16
diaspora, Orthodox, 125–6, 162;
   Russian, 37, 39, 63, 64, 143
Dionysius the Areopagite, 12
dogmatics, 124
Domos (publishers), 23
Dostoevsky, Feodor, 23, 134–5, 144,
   175
Dragoumis, Ion, 87, 175
Duby, Georges, 136, 175
Duquoc, Christian, 65, 175
Dušan, Stephen. See Stephen Dušan

ecclesia, 72, 85
ecclesiology, 114
ecumenism. See dialogue, ecumenical
ek-stasis, 15, 59, 79, 95–7, 99
Elements of Faith (by Christos
   Yannaras), 40
Eliot, T. S., 151, 175–6
Elytis, Odysseas, 163, 176
emperor, Byzantine, 138

Index